$\mathcal{L}$ENT *and* $\mathcal{E}$ASTER $\mathcal{W}$ISDOM

—— *from* ——

POPE JOHN PAUL II

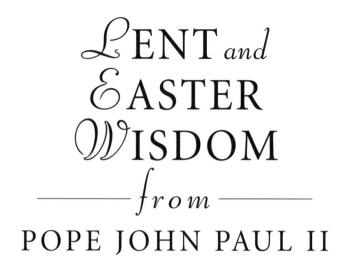

LENT and EASTER WISDOM
from
POPE JOHN PAUL II

Daily Scripture and Prayers Together
With John Paul II's Own Words

Compiled by John V. Kruse, PhD

Liguori

LIGUORI, MISSOURI

Imprimi Potest:
Thomas D. Picton, C.Ss.R.
Provincial, Denver Province
The Redemptorists

Published by Liguori Publications
Liguori, Missouri
www.liguori.org

Library of Congress Cataloging-in-Publication Data

John Paul II, 1920–2005.
Lent and Easter wisdom from John Paul II : daily scriptures and prayers together with John Paul II's own words / compiled by John V. Kruse.—1st ed.
    p.   cm.
Includes bibliographical references.
ISBN 978-0-7648-1412-9
    1. Lent—Prayer-books and devotions—English. 2. Holy week—Prayer-books and devotions—English. 3. Easter—Prayer-books and devotions—English. 4. Catholic Church—Prayer-books and devotions—English. I. Kruse, John V. II. Title.
BX2170.L4J64 2005
242'.34—dc22   2005029077

Acknowledgments of sources of quotations from John Paul II are listed on page 116.

Liguori Publications, a nonprofit corporation, is an apostolate of the Redemptorists. To learn more about the Redemptorists, visit *Redemptorists.com*.

Printed in the United States of America
11 10 09 08   5 4 3 2

Contents

Preface

DURING THE NEARLY TWENTY-SEVEN YEARS of his papacy, John Paul II frequently reminded Christians of their call to take up the cross and follow Christ. During the last years of his life, the world watched as John Paul II practiced in an especially poignant fashion the words he had preached as he bravely faced the increasingly burdensome effects of Parkinson's disease. John Paul II's health took a drastic decline during the last Lenten season of his life (2005). His body grew increasingly weak and his speech became more and more difficult for him, eventually leading to a tracheotomy. During Easter week, John Paul required a feeding tube and developed a high fever. On March 31, he celebrated the anointing of sick. As the lights burned in the papal apartments, thousands kept vigil in St. Peter's Square to pray for the ailing pontiff. On April 2, 2005 (Easter Saturday, Vigil of Second Sunday of Easter), John Paul II died with his last words reportedly being, "Let me go to the house of the Father."

John Paul II's last Lenten journey and celebration of Easter can serve as a model for all. With courageous determination, he embraced suffering and took up his cross to follow Jesus. He did so, however, with complete confidence that the resurrection of Jesus conquered death, pain, and suffering once and for all. May his words contained in this book inspire all to follow his moving example of Christian discipleship.

JOHN V. KRUSE
SAINT LOUIS, MISSOURI

Introduction

MOST CATHOLICS seem to be aware that the forty-day period before the feast of Easter, Lent—which comes from the Anglo-Saxon word *lencten*, meaning "spring"—is a time marked by particular rituals, such as the reception of ashes on Ash Wednesday or the practice of fasting and almsgiving. What is the significance of these rituals, and how do we observe the Lenten season today?

A BRIEF HISTORY OF LENT

In the first three centuries of Christian experience, preparation for the Easter feast usually covered a period of one or two days, perhaps a week at the most. Saint Irenaeus of Lyons (ca. AD 140–202) even speaks of a *forty-hour* preparation for Easter.

The first reference to Lent as a period of forty days' preparation occurs in the teachings of the First Council of Nicaea in AD 325. By the end of the fourth century, a Lenten period of forty days was established and accepted.

In its early development, Lent quickly became associated with the sacrament of baptism, since Easter was the great baptismal feast. Those who were preparing to be baptized participated in the season of Lent in preparation for the reception of the sacrament of baptism. Eventually, those who were already baptized considered it important to join these candidates preparing for baptism in their preparations for Easter. The customs and practices of Lent, as we know them today, soon took hold.

LENT AS A JOURNEY

Lent is often portrayed as a journey, from one point in time to another point in time. The concept of journey is obvious for those experiencing the Rite of Christian Initiation of Adults (RCIA), a four-stage program of baptismal preparation that culminates during Lent and ends during the Easter Vigil.

But Lenten preparation is not limited to those who are preparing to be baptized and join the Church. For many Catholics, Lent is a journey that is measured from Ash Wednesday through Easter Sunday, but, more accurately, Lent is measured from Ash Wednesday to the beginning of the period known as the Triduum.

Triduum begins after the Mass on Holy Thursday, continues through Good Friday, and concludes with the Easter Vigil on Holy Saturday. Lent officially ends with the proclamation of the *Exsultet*, "Rejoice, O Heavenly Powers," during the Mass of Holy Saturday.

By whatever yardstick the journey is measured, it is not only the time that is important but the essential experiences of the journey that are necessary for a full appreciation of what is being celebrated.

The Lenten journey is also a process of spiritual growth and, as such, presumes movement from one state of being to another state. For example, some people may find themselves troubled and anxious at the beginning of Lent as a result of a life choice or an unanswered question, and, at the end of Lent, they may fully expect a sense of conversion, a sense of peace, or perhaps simply understanding and acceptance. Therefore, Lent is a movement from one point of view to another or, perhaps, from one interpretation of life to a different interpretation.

Scripture, psalms, prayers, rituals, practices, and penance are the components of the Lenten journey. Each component, tried and tested by years of tradition, is one of the "engines" that drives the season and which brings the weary spiritual traveler to the joys of Easter.

PENITENTIAL NATURE OF LENT

A popular understanding of Lent is that it is a penitential period during which people attempt to become more sensitive to the role of sin in their lives. Lenten sermons will speak of personal sin, coming to an awareness of the sins of others and the effect such sin might have, and, finally, the sin that can be found within our larger society and culture. Awareness of sin, however, is balanced by an emphasis on the love and acceptance that God still has for humanity, despite the sinful condition in which we still find ourselves.

The practice of meditation of the passion of the Lord, his suffering, and his death is also seen as part of the penitential experience of Lent. There is also a traditional concern for the reception of the sacrament of reconciliation during Lent. Originally, the sacrament of reconciliation was celebrated before Lent began, the penance was imposed on Ash Wednesday, and performed during the entire forty-day period.

SUMMONS TO PENITENTIAL LIVING

"Jesus came to Galilee, proclaiming the good news of God, and saying, 'The time is fulfilled, and the kingdom of God has come near; repent, and believe in the good news'" (Mark 1:14–15). This call to conversion announces the solemn opening of Lent. Participants are marked with ashes, and the words, "Repent, and believe in the good news," are prayed. This blessing is understood as a personal acceptance of the desire to take on the life of penance for the sake of the gospel.

The example of Jesus in the desert for forty days—a time during which he fasted and prayed—is imitated. It is time to center attention on conversion. During Lent, the expectation is to examine our lives and, through the practice of prayer, fasting, and works of charity, seek to conform our lives to Christ's. For some, this conversion will be a turning from sin to grace. For others, it will be a gracious turning toward the mystery of God in Christ. Whatever the pattern chosen by a particular pilgrim for an observance of Lent, it is hoped that this book will provide a useful support in the effort.

PART I

~~~~~~

READINGS *for* LENT

DAY 1

Ash Wednesday

BEGINNING THE LENTEN JOURNEY

*R*emember, you are dust and to dust you will return. The traditional rite of distributing ashes...suggests the transitory nature of earthly life: everything passes and is destined to die. We are wayfarers in this world, wayfarers who must never forget their true and final destination: heaven....In dying on the cross, Jesus opened the way for every human being.

The entire Ash Wednesday liturgy helps us to focus on this fundamental truth of faith and spurs us to undertake a resolute journey of personal renewal. We must change our way of thinking and acting, set our gaze firmly on the face of Christ crucified and make his Gospel our daily rule of life. *Turn away from sin and be faithful to the Gospel*: let this be our Lenten program, as we enter an atmosphere of prayerful listening to the Spirit.

GENERAL AUDIENCE, FEBRUARY 28, 2001 (ASH WEDNESDAY)

From Dust to Eternal Life

Thus it is written, "The first man, Adam, became a living being"; the last Adam became a life-giving spirit. But it is not the spiritual that is first, but the physical, and then the spiritual. The first man was from the earth, a man of dust; the second man is from heaven. As was the man of dust, so are those who are of the dust; and as is the man of heaven, so are those who are of heaven. Just as we have borne the image of the man of dust, we will also bear the image of the man of heaven.

1 CORINTHIANS 15:45–49

Prayer

Loving God, as I begin this Lenten journey, I ask you to take me by the hand. I cannot see the road that leads to the joy of Easter. Not knowing what to expect, I am apprehensive as I set out. But I trust in you. Help me to make this a season of true conversion in my life. When we celebrate the resurrection of Jesus at Easter, I also want to celebrate the new life I have found in you through the penitential journey I now undertake. I know it will be a long, tough journey, but I entrust that journey to you with the single step that I take today.

Lenten Action

Write a short prayer telling God how you personally hope to benefit from this Lenten season. It need not be more than three lines. Place the prayer somewhere you will see it frequently during Lent.

DAY 2

Thursday After Ash Wednesday

THE PATH TO JERUSALEM

Behold, we are going up to Jerusalem (Mark 10:33). With these words, the Lord invites the disciples to journey with him on the path that leads from Galilee to the place where he will complete his redemptive mission. This journey to Jerusalem, which the Evangelists present as the crowning moment of the earthly journey of Jesus, is the model for the Christian who is committed to following the Master on the way of the Cross. Christ also invites the men and women of today to "go up to Jerusalem." He does so with special force during Lent, which is a favorable time to convert and restore full communion with him by sharing intimately in the mystery of his Death and Resurrection.

LENTEN MESSAGE 2001

SHARING IN CHRIST'S DEATH

Very truly, I tell you, unless a grain of wheat falls into the earth and dies, it remains just a single grain; but if it dies, it bears much fruit. Those who love their life lose it, and those who hate their life in this world will keep it for eternal life. Whoever serves me must follow me, and where I am, there will my servant be also. Whoever serves me, the Father will honor.

JOHN 12:24–26

PRAYER

Christ Jesus, my inclination is to jump from Ash Wednesday to Easter. I would rather not go through what lies in between. I know this feeling is not unnatural given that you, too, asked for the cup of your sacrifice to pass by you (see Matthew 26:39). This Lenten season, give me the strength to do all that I need to do to follow you on the path to Jerusalem. I know that I must suffer and die with you if I am to rise with you on Easter. Help me to die to myself, Lord, so that I might live with you.

LENTEN ACTION

How do you need to die to yourself this Lenten season? Is there an area of your life you need to give up in order to draw closer to Christ? Identify what is holding you back from giving yourself fully to Christ and commit to doing what it takes to break down this obstacle. Often, pride prevents us from placing ourselves fully in Christ's hands. We want to be in control of our own lives. Today, make a conscious effort to surrender your will to Christ. When you need to make a decision, ask Jesus what he would want you to do. Follow what you believe is Christ's will, even if this may involve some discomfort (or a "dying to self") on your part.

DAY 3

Friday After Ash Wednesday

THE COMMAND TO LOVE

*T*he greatest light comes from the commandment to love God and neighbor. In this commandment, human freedom finds its most complete realization. Freedom is for love: its realization through love can reach heroic proportions. Christ speaks of "laying down his life" for his friends, for other human beings. In the history of Christianity, many people in different ways have "laid down their lives" for their neighbor, and they have done so in order to follow the example of Christ. This is particularly true in the case of martyrs, whose testimony has accompanied Christianity right up to the present day. The twentieth century was the great century of Christian martyrs, and this is true both in the Catholic Church and in other Churches and ecclesial communities.

MEMORY AND IDENTITY

LOVING AS WE HAVE BEEN LOVED

"This is my commandment, that you love one another as I have loved you. No one has greater love than this, to lay down one's life for one's friends. You are my friends if you do what I command you."

JOHN 15:12–14

PRAYER

Lord God, you have commanded me to love you and my neighbor. The entire purpose of my life is to love. This seems simple, yet I know that at times my heart is slow to follow. Shape a loving heart in me, Lord, so that I might love you more dearly and serve my neighbor more generously. Teach me to love as you have loved me.

LENTEN ACTION

Purposely set aside your normal routine and preoccupations for a short period in order to spend time with a family member or a friend.

DAY 4

Saturday After Ash Wednesday

A TIME FOR LISTENING

*H*ow should we respond to the invitation to conversion that Jesus addresses to us in this time of Lent? How can there be a serious change in our life? First of all, we must open our hearts to the penetrating call that comes to us from the Liturgy. The time of preparation for Easter is a providential gift from the Lord and a precious opportunity to draw closer to him, turning inward to listen to his promptings deep within.

LENTEN MESSAGE 2001

HEARING THE LORD'S VOICE

Now the boy Samuel was ministering to the LORD under Eli. The word of the LORD was rare in those days; visions were not widespread.

At that time Eli, whose eyesight had begun to grow dim so that he could not see, was lying down in his room; the lamp of God had not yet gone out, and Samuel was lying down in the temple of the LORD, where the ark of God was. Then the LORD called, "Samuel! Samuel!" and he said, "Here I am!" and ran to Eli, and said, "Here I am, for you called me." But he said, "I did not call; lie down again." So he went and lay down. The LORD called again, "Samuel!" Samuel got up and went to Eli, and said, "Here I am, for you called me." But he said, "I did not call, my son; lie down again." Now Samuel did not yet know the LORD, and the word of the LORD had not yet been revealed to him. The LORD called Samuel again, a third time. And he got up and went to Eli, and said, "Here I am, for you called me." Then Eli perceived that the LORD was calling the boy. Therefore Eli said to Samuel, "Go, lie down; and if he calls you, you shall say, 'Speak, LORD, for your servant is listening.'" So Samuel went and lay down in his place. Now the LORD came and stood there, calling as before, "Samuel! Samuel!" And Samuel said, "Speak, for your servant is listening."

1 SAMUEL 3:1–10

PRAYER

Patient God, often I complain that you don't speak to me. Deep down, I know the problem is that I am not listening. Sometimes there is so much noise around me that it is hard to hear your voice. Help me to shut out the racket in my life so that I can better hear you. Understand too, Lord, when I ask you to speak louder! May my increased efforts to listen to your voice aid me in my Lenten journey to deeper communion with you.

LENTEN ACTION

Go to a place where you can experience absolute silence for five to ten minutes. What does the Lord tell you during this time?

DAY 5

First Sunday in Lent

LEARNING DEPENDENCY ON GOD

𝒯he season of Lent recalls the forty years spent by Israel in the desert while on its way to the promised land. During that time the people experienced what it meant to live in tents, without a fixed abode, totally lacking security. How often they were tempted to return to Egypt, where at least there was a supply of bread even though it was the food of slaves. In the insecurity of the desert, God himself provided water and food for his people, protecting them from every danger. For the Hebrews, the experience of being total dependent on God thus became the path to freedom....

The Lenten season is meant to help believers, through a commitment to personal purification, to relive this same spiritual journey, by becoming more aware of poverty and of life's uncertainties, and by rediscovering the providential presence of the Lord....

LENTEN MESSAGE 1997

TRUSTING THE LORD

"Therefore I tell you, do not worry about your life, what you will eat or what you will drink, or about your body, what you will wear. Is not life more than food, and the body more than clothing? Look at the birds of the air; they neither sow nor reap nor gather into barns, and yet your heavenly Father feeds them. Are you not of more value than they? And can any of you by worrying add a single hour to your span of life? And why do you worry about clothing? Consider the lilies of the field, how they grow; they neither toil nor spin, yet I tell you, even Solomon in all his glory was not clothed like one of these. But if God so clothes the grass of the field…will he not much more clothe you— you of little faith? Therefore do not worry, saying, 'What will we eat?' or 'What will we drink?' or 'What will we wear?' For it is the Gentiles who strive for all these things; and indeed your heavenly Father knows that you need all these things. But strive first for the kingdom of God and his righteousness, and all these things will be given to you as well. So do not worry about tomorrow, for tomorrow will bring worries of its own. Today's trouble is enough for today."

MATTHEW 6:25–34

PRAYER

Benevolent God, my life is full of uncertainty. How will I make it from one day to the next? How will I get all of my work done? How will the bills be paid? How will I hold my family together? It is among these uncertainties, however, that I learn my dependence on you. I cannot do it alone; I need you. During this Lenten journey, help me to trust in you, Most Faithful God.

LENTEN ACTION

Place a worry in God's hands today. Let go of it and entrust it to his care.

DAY 6

Monday of the First Week of Lent

LETTING GO OF THE FAMILIAR

We must remember too that the promise [of a life greater than death] was made not just to Abraham, but to his descendants as well: that is, to us! During Lent, therefore, we bring to God all that is barren and dead in ourselves, all our sorrows and our sins, trusting that God who gave Sarah a son and who raised Jesus from the dead will turn all that is barren and dead in our lives into new and wonderful life. But this means that we must leave behind much that is familiar....

Because we live in a sinful world, Lent itself must become a kind of separation. We are called to leave behind our old ways of sin, which make our lives sterile and condemn us to spiritual death. Yet these sinful ways are often so deeply rooted in our lives that it is painful to leave them behind and set out for the land of blessing which God promises. This repentance is difficult; but it is the price that must be paid if we are to receive the blessing which the Father promises to those who listen to the voice of Jesus.

HOMILY AT MASS FOR THE PHILIPPINE COMMUNITY GATHERED AT THE BASILICA OF ST. PUDENZIANA, FEBRUARY 24, 2002 (SECOND SUNDAY OF LENT)

LEAVING BEHIND THE FAMILIAR AND FOLLOWING CHRIST

As he walked by the Sea of Galilee, he saw two brothers, Simon, who is called Peter, and Andrew his brother, casting a net into the sea— for they were fishermen. And he said to them, "Follow me, and I will make you fish for people." Immediately they left their nets and followed him. As he went from there, he saw two other brothers, James son of Zebedee and his brother John, in the boat with their father Zebedee, mending their nets, and he called them. Immediately they left the boat and their father, and followed him.

MATTHEW 4:18–22

PRAYER

Lord, you call me to a life beyond what I can imagine. I want to follow you, but sometimes it is hard to let go of the things in my life that make me feel comfortable, even if those are things that keep me from you and a more fulfilling life. As I let go of those things that keep a distance between us, help me to trust that you are leading me into a deeper, life-giving union with you. What I must let go of can never compare with what I have to gain!

LENTEN ACTION

Take a risk and trust God. Consciously get rid of one thing in your life (either material or mental) to which you have grown accustomed but that serves as a hindrance to your relationship with God.

DAY 7

Tuesday of the First Week of Lent

FINDING CHRIST IN OUR OWN SHORTCOMINGS

*T*rue disciples of Christ are conscious of their own weakness. For this reason they put all their trust in the grace of God and they accept it with undivided hearts, convinced that without Him they can do nothing (see John 15:5). What characterizes them and distinguishes them from others is not their talents or natural gifts. It is their firm determination to proceed as followers of Jesus. May you be imitators of them as they were of Christ!

MESSAGE FOR THE 18TH WORLD YOUTH DAY (APRIL 13, 2003), FROM THE VATICAN, MARCH 8, 2003

CHRIST'S STRENGTH REVEALED IN HUMAN WEAKNESS

Therefore, to keep me from being too elated, a thorn was given me in the flesh, a messenger of Satan to torment me, to keep me from being too elated. Three times I appealed to the Lord about this, that it would leave me, but he said to me, "My grace is sufficient for you, for power is made perfect in weakness." So, I will boast all the more gladly of my weaknesses, so that the power of Christ may dwell in me. Therefore I am content with weaknesses, insults, hardships, persecutions, and calamities for the sake of Christ; for whenever I am weak, then I am strong.

2 CORINTHIANS 12:7–10

PRAYER

Lord, there is no hiding it: I am far from perfect. I have many weaknesses. I fall many times on my spiritual journey. I praise you as you use my neediness and weakness to demonstrate your own strength and glory. Help me to remember that you can work great things through me—warts and all. I need only to follow you.

LENTEN ACTION

Identify one of your weaknesses. Place that weakness in God's hands. Think of a way that God may have used that weakness to demonstrate his own strength and glory.

DAY 8

Wednesday of the First Week of Lent

BE NOT AFRAID!

*A*t the end of the second millennium, we need, perhaps more than ever, the words of the Risen Christ: Be not afraid!… Peoples and nations of the entire world need to hear these words. Their conscience needs to grow in the certainty that Someone exists who holds in His hands the destiny of the passing world; Someone who holds the keys to death and the netherworld (see Revelation 1:18); Someone who is the Alpha and the Omega of human history (see Revelation 22:13)—be it the individual or collective history. And this Someone is Love (see 1 John 4:8, 16)— Love that became man, Love crucified and risen, Love unceasingly present among men. It is Eucharistic Love. It is the infinite source of communion. He alone can give the ultimate assurance when He says, Be not afraid!

CROSSING THE THRESHOLD OF HOPE, 1994

THE PEACE THAT CHRIST GIVES

"Peace I leave with you; my peace I give to you. I do not give to you as the world gives. Do not let your hearts be troubled, and do not let them be afraid."

JOHN 14:27

PRAYER

Lord Jesus, there seems to be so much to be afraid of in our modern world. When I am afraid, help me to remember that with you at my side, I can face anything. I know that you have taken all fear upon yourself on the cross. I ask for the courage and strength to face all of my fears. Fill me with the peace that only your love can bring.

LENTEN ACTION

Reflect on what it is that you most fear. Write the fear down. Entrust that fear to Jesus by placing it on or near a crucifix, or by burning it.

DAY 9

Thursday of the First Week of Lent

BECAUSE OUR LIVES ARE GIFTS,
WE MUST MAKE GIFTS OF OUR LIVES

*Y*ou received without paying, give without pay" (Matthew 10:8). May these words of the Gospel echo in the heart of all Christian communities on their penitential pilgrimage to Easter. May Lent, recalling the mystery of the Lord's Death and Resurrection, lead all Christians to marvel in their heart of hearts at the greatness of such a gift. Yes! We have received without pay. Is not our entire life marked by God's kindness? The beginning of life and its marvelous development: this is a gift. And because it is gift, life can never be regarded as a possession or as private property, even if the capabilities we now have to improve the quality of life can lead us to think that man is the "master" of life....

"What do you have," Saint Paul asks, "that you did not receive?" (1 Corinthians 4:7). The demand which follows this recognition is that of loving our brothers and sisters, and of dedicating ourselves to them. The more needy they are, the more urgent the believer's duty to serve them. Does not God permit human need so that by responding to the needs of others we may learn to free ourselves from our egoism and to practice authentic Gospel love?...

Dear Brothers and Sisters! Let this be how we prepare to live this Lent: in practical generosity towards the poorest of our brothers and sisters!...[W]hat we give to others is our response to the many gifts which the Lord continues to give to us. We have received without paying, let us give without pay!

LENTEN MESSAGE 2002

LOVE IN ACTION

We know love by this, that he laid down his life for us—and we ought to lay down our lives for one another. How does God's love abide in anyone who has the world's goods and sees a brother or sister in need and yet refuses help? Little children, let us love, not in word or speech, but in truth and action.

1 JOHN 3:16–18

PRAYER

Generous God, I realize that my entire life is a gift from you. I deserve nothing from you and yet you have given all to me, even the gift of your own Son. This Lenten season, help me to look beyond my own selfish wants and desires so that I may see the needs of others. Give me the strength, courage, and patience to give of myself, even when I don't have the time or energy.

LENTEN ACTION

Make a special donation today and help someone in need. This can be a gift of your time, talent, or financial resources. As you make this donation, consciously thank God for all that he has given you.

DAY 10

Friday of the First Week of Lent

TAKING SERIOUSLY THE CALL
TO FORGIVE AND LOVE ONE'S ENEMIES

There are Christians who think they can dispense with this unceasing spiritual effort [of personal conversion], because they do not see the urgency of standing before the truth of the Gospel. Lest their way of life be upset, they seek to take words like "Love your enemies, do good to those who hate you" (Luke 6:27) and render them empty and innocuous. For these people, it is extremely difficult to accept such words and to translate them into consistent patterns of behavior. They are in fact words which, if taken seriously, demand a radical conversion. On the other hand, when we are offended or hurt, we are tempted to succumb to the psychological impulses of self-pity and revenge, ignoring Jesus' call to love our enemy. Yet the daily experiences of human life show very clearly how much forgiveness and reconciliation are indispensable if there is to be genuine renewal, both personal and social. This applies not only to interpersonal relationships, but also to relationships between communities and nations.

LENTEN MESSAGE 2001

AGENTS OF PEACE

"But I say to you that listen, Love your enemies, do good to those who hate you, bless those who curse you, pray for those who abuse you. If anyone strikes you on the cheek, offer the other also; and from anyone who takes away your coat do not withhold even your shirt. Give to everyone who begs from you; and if anyone takes away your goods, do not ask for them again. Do to others as you would have them do to you. If you love those who love you, what credit is that to you? For even sinners love those who love them. If you do good to those who do good to you, what credit is that to you? For even sinners do the same. If you lend to those from whom you hope to receive, what credit is that to you? Even sinners lend to sinners, to receive as much again. But love your enemies, do good, and lend, expecting nothing in return. Your reward will be great, and you will be children of the Most High; for he is kind to the ungrateful and the wicked. Be merciful, just as your Father is merciful."

LUKE 6:27–36

PRAYER

Loving God, you really know how to challenge me. You ask that I forgive those who have wronged me and to seek reconciliation wherever I can. Often, I would rather hold a grudge and feel sorry for myself. You have shown, however, that I can make the world a better place by forgiving wrongs committed against me and by seeking forgiveness for wrongs I have committed. The peace of the world is built on the peace of individual relationships. Help me to be an agent of your peace in the world.

LENTEN ACTION

Reflect on a grudge or hurt you may be holding. Make an effort to forgive and to reach out to the person who may have wronged you. If you have harmed another, ask for that person's forgiveness. Do one small thing today to bring Christ's peace into the world.

DAY 11

Saturday of the First Week of Lent

FREED FROM THE SLAVERY OF SIN

*W*e were dead through sin (see Ephesians 2:5): this is how Saint Paul describes the situation of man without Christ. This is why the Son of God wished to unite himself to human nature, ransoming it from the slavery of sin and death.

This is a slavery which man experiences every day, as he perceives its deep roots in his own heart (see Matthew 7:11). Sometimes it shows itself in dramatic and unusual ways, as happened in the course of the great tragedies of the twentieth century, which deeply marked the lives of countless communities and individuals, the victims of cruel violence. Forced deportations, the systematic elimination of peoples, contempt for the fundamental rights of the person: these are the tragedies which even today humiliate humanity. In daily life too we see all sorts of forms of fraud, hatred, the destruction of others, and lies of which man is both the victim and source. Humanity is marked by sin....

In the face of the darkness of sin and man's incapacity to free himself on his own, there appears in all its splendor the saving work of Christ.... Christ is the Lamb who has taken upon himself the sin of the world (see John 1:29). He shared in human life "unto death, even death on a cross" (Philippians 2:8), to ransom mankind from the slavery of evil and restore humanity to its original dignity as children of God. This is the paschal mystery in which we are reborn....In the Risen Lord, death's power is broken and mankind is enabled, through faith, to enter into communion with God. To those who believe, God's very life is given, through the action of the Holy Spirit, the "first gift to those who believe" (*Eucharistic Prayer IV*). Thus the redemption accomplished on the Cross renews the universe and brings about the reconciliation of God and man, and of people with one another.

LENTEN MESSAGE 2000

FREED CHILDREN OF GOD

For all who are led by the Spirit of God are children of God. For you did not receive a spirit of slavery to fall back into fear, but you have received a spirit of adoption. When we cry, "Abba! Father!" it is that very Spirit bearing witness with our spirit that we are children of God, and if children, then heirs, heirs of God and joint heirs with Christ—if, in fact, we suffer with him so that we may also be glorified with him.

ROMANS 8:14–17

PRAYER

Compassionate God, the evidence of sin is apparent throughout the world. On the global scene, there is so much suffering and violence. Through the power of the cross, drive this evil from the world. On a personal level, I feel weighed down by my own sinfulness. I yearn to be freed from the shackles of sin that hold me back from living the life of fullness to which you call me. While I cannot do this on my own, I know you have sent your own Son to free me from sin and to reconcile myself with you. Please strengthen my faith so that I might recognize the freeing power of Jesus' love for me.

LENTEN ACTION

At some point this Lent, celebrate the freeing grace of the sacrament of reconciliation. You may have put it off in the past. Make a commitment today to embrace it this Lenten season.

DAY 12

Second Sunday of Lent

OUR ULTIMATE GOAL

The blessing which we receive in Christ breaks down for us the wall of time and opens to us the door which leads us to a full share in the life of God. "Blessed are those invited to the wedding-banquet of the Lamb" (Revelation 19:9): we cannot forget that in this banquet—anticipated in the Sacrament of the Eucharist—our life finds its final goal. Christ has gained for us not only new dignity in our life on earth, but above all the new dignity of the children of God, called to share eternal life with him. Lent invites us to overcome the temptation of seeing the realities of this world as definitive and to recognize that "our homeland is in heaven" (Philippians 3:20).

LENTEN MESSAGE 1999

FAITH AT THE CENTER OF OUR LIVES

But as for you, man of God, shun all this; pursue righteousness, godliness, faith, love, endurance, gentleness. Fight the good fight of the faith; take hold of the eternal life, to which you were called and for which you made the good confession in the presence of many witnesses. In the presence of God, who gives life to all things, and of Christ Jesus, who in his testimony before Pontius Pilate made the good confession, I charge you to keep the commandment without spot or blame until the manifestation of our Lord Jesus Christ, which he will bring about at the right time—he who is the blessed and only Sovereign, the King of kings and Lord of lords. It is he alone who has immortality and dwells in unapproachable light, whom no one has ever seen or can see; to him be honor and eternal dominion. Amen.

1 TIMOTHY 6:11–16

PRAYER

Faithful God, it is you who gives meaning to my life. Sometimes I lose sight of this fact. I try to find meaning in what I do and what I have. I become distracted by things of the world. If I put my relationship with you first, all areas of my life will fall into place. Let everything I do—all my daily choices and decisions—be directed toward my ultimate goal: eternal life with you.

LENTEN ACTION

Do something concrete to show that your relationship with God is the first priority in your life. Abstain from something in which you might otherwise indulge. For example, instead of watching a television show or going shopping, go for a walk just to spend time in prayer with God. Perhaps give something that you cherish to charity or to a loved one.

DAY 13

Monday of the Second Week of Lent

SWIMMING AGAINST THE TIDE

*O*f course, the message that the cross communicates is not easy to understand in our day and age in which material well-being and conveniences are offered and sought as priority values. But you, dear young people, do not be afraid to proclaim the Gospel of the cross in every circumstance. Do not be afraid to swim against the tide!

HOMILY, APRIL 4, 2004 (PALM SUNDAY),
19TH WORLD YOUTH DAY

LIVING COUNTER-CULTURALLY

I appeal to you therefore, brothers and sisters, by the mercies of God, to present your bodies as a living sacrifice, holy and acceptable to God, which is your spiritual worship. Do not be conformed to this world, but be transformed by the renewing of your minds, so that you may discern what is the will of God—what is good and acceptable and perfect.

ROMANS 12:1–2

PRAYER

Lord, there is a lot in popular culture that draws me away from you. Often, I feel pressure to conform to the ways of the world that are not your ways. I want to be liked and I want to have fun with everyone else. I know you call me to stand by you, even when doing so may not be fun or popular. Sometimes, this is how I am called to show my love for you. Give me the courage, Lord, to do what is right, even when this means swimming against the tide.

LENTEN ACTION

How is God calling you to swim against the tide in your own life? Make an effort to reach out to someone who is not popular.

DAY 14

Tuesday of the Second Week of Lent

MEETING JESUS FACE TO FACE

*T*he desire to see Jesus dwells deep in the heart of each man and each woman....[A]llow Jesus to gaze into your eyes so that the desire to see the Light, and to experience the splendor of the Truth, may grow within you. Whether we are aware of it or not, God has created us because he loves us and so that we in turn may love him. This is the reason for the unquenchable nostalgia for God that man preserves in his heart: "Your face, Lord, do I seek. Do not hide your face from me" (Psalm 27:8–9). That Face—we know—was revealed to us by God in Jesus Christ.

...[D]on't you too wish to contemplate the beauty of that Face? That is the question I address to you....Don't be too hasty in your reply. First of all, create a silence within yourselves. Allow this ardent desire to see God emerge from the depth of your hearts, a desire that is sometimes stifled by the distractions of the world and by the allurements of pleasures. Allow this desire to emerge and you will have the wonderful experience of meeting Jesus. Christianity is not simply a doctrine: it is an encounter in faith with God made present in our history through the incarnation of Jesus.

HOMILY, APRIL 4, 2004 (PALM SUNDAY),
19TH WORLD YOUTH DAY

THE FACES OF JESUS

Six days later, Jesus took with him Peter and James and his brother John and led them up a high mountain, by themselves. And he was transfigured before them, and his face shone like the sun, and his clothes became dazzling white.

MATTHEW 17:1–2

Then the high priest tore his clothes and said, "He has blasphemed! Why do we still need witnesses? You have now heard his blasphemy. What is your verdict?" They answered, "He deserves death." Then they spat in his face and struck him; and some slapped him....

MATTHEW 26:65–67

PRAYER

Jesus, my Brother, I long to see your face, for in your face I see the face of God as well as the face of all that I am called to be. I receive my ultimate comfort in life when I can see your face. I have no better friend than you. Help me to see your face whenever and wherever I can, especially in the faces of the needy around me.

LENTEN ACTION

Take five minutes to pray with an icon or other picture of Jesus while concentrating on his face. What do you see in his face that strikes you? What is Jesus trying to tell you?

DAY 15

Wednesday of the Second Week of Lent

SEEING CHRIST IN THE FACE OF THE POOR

The fruit of...a courageous ascetical journey can only be a greater openness to the needs of our neighbor. Those who love the Lord cannot close their eyes to individuals and peoples who are tried by suffering and poverty. After contemplating the face of the crucified Lord, how can we not recognize him and serve him in those who are suffering and abandoned? Jesus himself, who invites us to stay with him watching and praying, also asks us to love him in our brothers and sisters, remembering that *as you did it to one of the least of these my brethren, you did it to me* (Matthew 25:40). The fruit of a Lent intensely lived will thus be a greater and more universal love.

GENERAL AUDIENCE, FEBRUARY 28, 2001 (ASH WEDNESDAY)

THE FINAL JUDGMENT

"Then the king will say to those at his right hand, 'Come, you that are blessed by my Father, inherit the kingdom prepared for you from the foundation of the world; for I was hungry and you gave me food, I was thirsty and you gave me something to drink, I was a stranger and you welcomed me, I was naked and you gave me clothing, I was sick and you took care of me, I was in prison and you visited me.' Then the righteous will answer him, 'Lord, when was it that we saw you hungry and gave you food, or thirsty and gave you something to drink? And when was it that we saw you a stranger and welcomed you, or naked and gave you clothing? And when was it that we saw you sick or in prison and visited you?' And the king will answer them, 'Truly I tell you, just as you did it to one of the least of these who are members of my family, you did it to me."

MATTHEW 25:34–40

PRAYER

Ultimately, Lord, you say we will be judged according to how we treat the least among us. The way we treat them is, in fact, the way we treat you. At times, I go through life with blinders on. I do not want to see those in need. By turning my back on them, I am turning my back on you. This Lenten season, help me to open my eyes to see my responsibility to help those who are less fortunate—whether in my immediate neighborhood or on the other side of the world. Give me a generous heart.

LENTEN ACTION

Reflect on the following: What is your attitude toward those in need? Are you more concerned about helping or assigning blame to them for their state in life? Make a donation to a charitable organization. Do not put it off. Make the commitment today.

DAY 16

Thursday of the Second Week of Lent

THE SPIRITUALITY OF COMMUNION

A spirituality of communion indicates above all the heart's contemplation of the mystery of the Trinity dwelling in us, and whose light we must also be able to see shining on the face of the brothers and sisters around us. A spirituality of communion also means an ability to think of our brothers and sisters in faith within the profound unity of the Mystical Body, and therefore as "those who are a part of me." This makes us able to share their joys and sufferings, to sense their desires and attend to their needs, to offer them deep and genuine friendship. A spirituality of communion implies also the ability to see what is positive in others, to welcome it and prize it as a gift from God: not only as a gift for the brother or sister who has received it directly, but also as a "gift for me." A spirituality of communion means, finally, to know how to "make room" for our brothers and sisters, bearing "each other's burdens" (Galatians 6:2) and resisting the selfish temptations which constantly beset us and provoke competition, careerism, distrust and jealousy. Let us have no illusions: unless we follow this spiritual path, external structures of communion will serve very little purpose. They would become mechanisms without a soul, "masks" of communion rather than its means of expression and growth.

NOVO MILLENNIO INEUNTE
(AT THE BEGINNING OF THE THIRD MILLENNIUM), JANUARY 6, 2001

BEING ONE BODY

For just as the body is one and has many members, and all the members of the body, though many, are one body, so it is with Christ. For in the one Spirit we were all baptized into one body—Jews or Greeks, slaves or free—and we were all made to drink of one Spirit. Indeed, the body does not consist of one member but of many....If one member suffers, all suffer together with it; if one member is honored, all rejoice together with it.

1 CORINTHIANS 12:12–13, 26

PRAYER

Triune God, so often it easy to see myself in isolation from others. I tell myself that I have my own interests to protect. I don't want others interfering in my life, and I certainly don't want to be bothered by the problems of others. Teach me that we are all members of one body in Jesus. Help me to see the good in others. Help me to recognize others as the gifts that they are in my life. End our divisions, God, for we need one another as we journey on our common pilgrimage to eternal union with you.

LENTEN ACTION

Is there someone who absolutely irritates you? Find a good quality in that person and thank God for that gift.

DAY 17

Friday of the Second Week of Lent

RETURNED TO DIGNITY BY GOD'S MERCY

*M*ercy—as Christ has presented it in the parable of the prodigal son—has the interior form of the love that in the New Testament is called agape. This love is able to reach down to every prodigal son, to every human misery, and above all to every form of moral misery, to sin. When this happens, the person who is the object of mercy does not feel humiliated, but rather found again and "restored to value." The father first and foremost expresses to him his joy that he has been "found again" and that he has "returned to life." This joy indicates a good that has remained intact: even if he is a prodigal, a son does not cease to be truly his father's son; it also indicates a good that has been found again, which in the case of the prodigal son was his return to the truth about himself.

DIVES IN MISERICORDIA (RICH IN MERCY), NOVEMBER 30, 1980

The Merciful Love of the Father

Then Jesus said, "There was a man who had two sons. The younger of them said to his father, "Father, give me the share of the property that will belong to me.' So he divided his property between them. A few days later the younger son gathered all he had and traveled to a distant country, and there he squandered his property in dissolute living....So he set off and went to his father. But while he was still far off, his father saw him and was filled with compassion; he ran and put his arms around him and kissed him. Then the son said to him, 'Father, I have sinned against heaven and before you; I am no longer worthy to be called your son.' But the father said to his slaves, 'Quickly, bring out a robe—the best one—and put it on him; put a ring on his finger and sandals on his feet. And get the fatted calf and kill it, and let us eat and celebrate; for this son of mine was dead and is alive again; he was lost and is found!' And they began to celebrate."

LUKE 15:11–13, 20–24

Prayer

Merciful Father, I sometimes turn from you and reject your love. I think I can make it on my own and I stubbornly refuse to follow you. If it were not for your mercy, I would be forever lost. Help me to remember that you are always waiting to welcome me back and to restore my great dignity as your child.

Lenten Action

Show thanks for God's mercy in your life by reflecting it. When someone wrongs you today, excuse him or her...even before he or she asks for forgiveness.

DAY 18

Saturday of the Second Week of Lent

LENT: A TIME OF THANKSGIVING

*L*ent is the favorable time to offer to the Lord sincere thanks for the wonders he has done for humanity in every age, and especially in the Redemption when he did not spare his own Son (see Romans 8:32).

LENTEN MESSAGE 1999

On the Cross, Jesus died for each one of us. The Cross, therefore, is the greatest and most eloquent sign of his merciful love, the one sign of salvation for every generation and for all humanity.

HOMILY, APRIL 4, 2004 (PALM SUNDAY),
19TH WORLD YOUTH DAY

GIVING THANKS FOR ALL OF GOD'S GIFTS

Rejoice always, pray without ceasing, give thanks in all circumstances; for this is the will of God in Christ Jesus for you. Do not quench the Spirit. Do not despise the words of prophets, but test everything; hold fast to what is good; abstain from every form of evil.

1 THESSALONIANS 5:16–22

"For God so loved the world that he gave his only Son, so that everyone who believes in him may not perish but may have eternal life."

JOHN 3:16

PRAYER

Benevolent God, during the Lenten season I sometimes focus on the negative around me instead of the good. I am so focused on penitence and personal conversion that I forget to notice your abundant blessings. Help me to be ever-mindful of all the goodness with which you have blessed my life. May I always be thankful for all you have given me—regardless if things are going well or poorly in my life. Thank you most of all the supreme display of your love for me: the gift of your Son.

LENTEN ACTION

Look around you and reflect on your life. Can you see things that you never noticed before, for which you should be thankful? Offer thanks to God for these things.

DAY 19

Third Sunday of Lent

FINDING CHRIST IN THE CHURCH

*D*o not forget to seek Christ and to recognize his presence in the Church, which is like the continuation of his saving action in time and space. It is in the Church and through her that Jesus continues to make himself visible today and to allow humanity to come to him. In your parishes, movements and communities, be welcoming to one another in order to build communion among yourselves. This is the visible sign of the presence of Christ in the Church, in spite of being so often blurred by human sin.

MESSAGE FOR THE 19TH WORLD YOUTH DAY (APRIL 4, 2004), FROM THE VATICAN, FEBRUARY 24, 2004

CHRIST'S BODY: THE CHURCH

God put this power to work in Christ when he raised him from the dead and seated him at his right hand in the heavenly places, far above all rule and authority and power and dominion, and above every name that is named, not only in this age but also in the age to come. And he has put all things under his feet and has made him the head over all things for the church, which is his body, the fullness of him who fills all in all.

EPHESIANS 1:20–23

PRAYER

Lord Jesus, we, your Church, are your continued presence in the world. We, your body, are called to bring your Good News to all and to bring all into loving communion with you. Help us to never undervalue your presence in the Church. It is in your Church that we find the means of salvation that strengthen us for our spiritual journey. May we always use the gifts that you have given us for the good of your Church. Bless your Church, so that it may truly be the universal sacrament of salvation.

LENTEN ACTION

Take a step to become more active in your parish. Use the gifts God has given you for the benefit of Christ's body, the Church.

DAY 20

Monday of the Third Week of Lent

FIGHTING THE SPIRITUAL BATTLE

Watch and pray that you may not enter into temptation; the spirit indeed is willing, but the flesh is weak (Matthew 26:41). Let us be guided by these words of the Lord in a committed effort of conversion and spiritual renewal. In daily life there is a risk of being absorbed in material concerns and interests. Lent is an appropriate time for a reawakening of genuine faith, for a salutary renewal of our relationship with God, and for a more generous Gospel commitment. The means available to us are the same as always, but we must use them more intensely in these weeks: prayer, fasting and penance, as well as almsgiving, that is, the sharing of what we have with the needy. This personal and community journey of asceticism can be particularly difficult at times because of the secularized environment in which we live. But for this very reason our effort must be stronger and more determined.

GENERAL AUDIENCE, FEBRUARY 28, 2001 (ASH WEDNESDAY)

ALMSGIVING, PRAYING, AND FASTING IN A SPIRIT OF LOVE

"Beware of practicing your piety before others in order to be seen by them; for then you have no reward from your Father in heaven....

"[W]hen you give alms, do not let your left hand know what your right hand is doing, so that your alms may be done in secret; and your Father who sees in secret will reward you....

"[W]henever you pray, go into your room and shut the door and pray to your Father who is in secret; and your Father who sees in secret will reward you....

"[W]hen you fast, put oil on your head and wash your face, so that your fasting may be seen not by others but by your Father who is in secret; and your Father who sees in secret will reward you."

MATTHEW 6:1, 3–4, 6, 17–18

PRAYER

Lord, I am surrounded by temptations in my life. I often feel weak as I face them. You have made known to me weapons that I can use as I wage battles against temptation. May the practices of almsgiving, prayer, fasting and other forms of penance strengthen me spiritually and deepen my relationship with you. I want to "fight the good fight" (see 2 Timothy 4:7). Be my strength when I am weak.

LENTEN ACTION

Eat a smaller meal today than you ordinarily would or avoid snacking. Allow yourself to experience hunger. Let this experience make you mindful of your own spiritual hunger for God and of those in the world who do not choose to be hungry.

DAY 21

Tuesday of the Third Week of Lent

THE CALL FOR JUSTICE

*P*rayer and fasting, however, must be accompanied by works of justice; conversion must be translated into welcome and solidarity. The ancient Prophet warns: *Is not this the fast that I choose; to loose the bonds of wickedness, / to undo the thongs of the yoke, / to let the oppressed go free, /and to break every yoke?* (Isaiah 58, 6).

There will be no peace on earth while the oppression of peoples, social injustices and existing economic imbalances continue. Yet for the great and hoped for structural changes, extrinsic initiatives and mediations are not enough; above all, we need the unanimous conversion of hearts to love.

HOMILY AT LENTEN STATION IN THE BASILICA OF ST. SABINA, MARCH 5, 2003 (ASH WEDNESDAY)

No Justice, No Peace

> *The way of peace they do not know,*
> *and there is no justice in their paths.*
> *Their roads they have made crooked;*
> *no one who walks in them knows peace.*

ISAIAH 59:8

> *He has told you, O mortal, what is good;*
> *and what does the* LORD *require of you*
> *but to do justice, and to love kindness,*
> *and to walk humbly with your God?*

MICAH 6:8

Prayer

Lord, I know that penitential acts are important this Lenten season, but you also call me to work for justice. Stir me, Lord, so that I am not apathetic to the injustices in the world around me. Lead me to deeper love of all people and help me to work for justice so that the world might know peace.

Lenten Action

Make an effort to learn more about an injustice happening in your own country or abroad. Share what you learn with at least one other person. What concrete step can you take to address this issue, if only in a small way? Write a letter to a government official asking him or her to address this injustice.

DAY 22

Wednesday of the Third Week of Lent

VALUING OUR ELDERLY

*I*t is upon this theme [the dignity of the elderly] that I would like to ask you to reflect during this Lent, in order to deepen the awareness of the role that the elderly are called to play in society and in the Church, and thus to prepare your hearts for the loving welcome that should always be reserved for them. Thanks to the contribution of science and medicine, one sees in society today a lengthening of the human life span and a subsequent increase in the number of elderly. This demands a more specific attention to the world of so-called "old" age, in order to help its members to live their full potential by placing them at the service of the entire community. The care of the elderly, above all when they pass through difficult moments, must be of great concern to all the faithful, especially in the ecclesial communities of Western societies, where the problem is particularly present....

How important it is to rediscover this mutual enrichment between different generations! The Lenten Season, with its strong call to conversion and solidarity, leads us this year to focus on these important themes which concern everyone. What would happen if the People of God yielded to a certain current mentality that considers these people, our brothers and sisters, as almost useless when they are reduced in their capacities due to the difficulties of age or sickness? Instead, how different the community would be, if, beginning with the family, it tries always to remain open and welcoming towards them.

LENTEN MESSAGE 2005

HONORING OUR SENIORS

You shall rise before the aged, and defer to the old; and you shall fear your God: I am the LORD.

LEVITICUS 19:32

PRAYER

Lord, I live in a culture that idolizes what is new and throws away what is old. Unfortunately, this sometimes extends to people as well. Youth is seen as the ideal while the elderly are seen as having little to contribute to society. Teach me to honor and respect those who are older than I am. Help me to value all that they have to offer, especially the wisdom that comes with years. May the example of their holiness lead me closer to you.

LENTEN ACTION

Take time to listen to the wisdom of someone older than you today. Make a special effort to let a senior citizen know how special he or she is.

DAY 23

Thursday of the Third Week of Lent

UNIVERSAL CALL TO HOLINESS

*S*ince Baptism is a true entry into the holiness of God through incorporation into Christ and the indwelling of his Spirit, it would be a contradiction to settle for a life of mediocrity, marked by a minimalist ethic and a shallow religiosity....

[T]his ideal of perfection must not be misunderstood as if it involved some kind of extraordinary existence, possible only for a few "uncommon heroes" of holiness. The ways of holiness are many, according to the vocation of each individual. I thank the Lord that in these years he has enabled me to beatify and canonize a large number of Christians, and among them many lay people who attained holiness in the most ordinary circumstances of life. The time has come to re-propose wholeheartedly to everyone this high standard of ordinary Christian living.

NOVO MILLENNIO INEUNTE
(AT THE BEGINNING OF THE THIRD MILLENNIUM), JANUARY 6, 2001

CALLED TO BE SAINTS

So then you are no longer strangers and aliens, but you are citizens with the saints and also members of the household of God, built upon the foundation of the apostles and prophets, with Christ Jesus himself as the cornerstone. In him the whole structure is joined together and grows into a holy temple in the Lord; in whom you also are built together spiritually into a dwelling place for God.

EPHESIANS 2:19–22

PRAYER

Lord, you call me to greatness. You call me to be numbered among your saints. Help me to remember that I do not have to do outstanding feats recognized by others in order to please you. All I have to do is live out your call to love wherever I am in my life. I just have to be the best "me" I can be. While this is all you ask of me, it is not always easy. Give me the strength to become the person you call me to be.

LENTEN ACTION

Mother Teresa is quoted as saying, "We can do no great things—only small things with great love." Live your call to holiness today in your own corner of the world. Whatever your vocation in life, go about your business motivated by great love. Make a special effort today to show others how much you love them.

DAY 24

Friday of the Third Week of Lent

MARY LEADS US TO CHRIST

You know that Christianity is not an opinion nor does it consist of empty words. Christianity is Christ! It is a Person, a Living Person! To meet Jesus, to love him and make him loved: this is the Christian vocation. Mary was given to you to help you enter into a more authentic and more personal relationship with Jesus. Through her example, Mary teaches you to gaze on him with love, for He has loved us first. Through her intercession, she forms in you a disciple's heart able to listen to her Son, who reveals the face of his Father and the true dignity of the human person.

MESSAGE FOR THE 18TH WORLD YOUTH DAY (APRIL 13, 2003),
FROM THE VATICAN, MARCH 8, 2003

Mary's Intercession

On the third day there was a wedding in Cana of Galilee, and the mother of Jesus was there. Jesus and his disciples had also been invited to the wedding. When the wine gave out, the mother of Jesus said to him, "They have no wine." And Jesus said to her, "Woman, what concern is that to you and to me? My hour has not yet come." His mother said to the servants, "Do whatever he tells you."

JOHN 2:1–5

Prayer

Mother Mary, you who were open to doing the Father's will, lead me closer to your Son this Lenten season. Teach me to obey his word and to follow him as you followed him: all the way to the foot of the cross. Pray for me, Holy Mother of God.

Lenten Action

Pray the sorrowful mysteries of the rosary.

DAY 25

Saturday of the Third Week of Lent

SHARING IN CHRIST'S REDEMPTIVE SUFFERING

*T*he Redeemer suffered in place of man and for man. Every man has his own share in the Redemption. Each one is also called to share in that suffering through which the Redemption was accomplished. He is called to share in that suffering through which all human suffering has also been redeemed. In bringing about the Redemption through suffering, Christ has also raised human suffering to the level of the Redemption. Thus each man, in his suffering, can also become a sharer in the redemptive suffering of Christ.

SALVIFICI DOLORIS (ON THE CHRISTIAN MEANING OF SUFFERING),
FEBRUARY 11, 1984

The adoration of the Cross directs us to a commitment that we cannot shirk: the mission that St. Paul expressed in these words: *[I]n my flesh I complete what is lacking in Christ's afflictions for the sake of his body, that is, the Church* (Colossians 1: 24). I also offer my sufferings so that God's plan may be completed and his Word spread among the peoples. I, in turn, am close to all who are tried by suffering at this time. I pray for each one of them.

MESSAGE TO THE PARTICIPANTS IN THE RITE OF THE WAY OF THE CROSS, MARCH 25, 2005

SUFFERING WITH CHRIST

We are afflicted in every way, but not crushed; perplexed, but not driven to despair; persecuted, but not forsaken; struck down, but not destroyed; always carrying in the body the death of Jesus, so that the life of Jesus may also be made visible in our bodies. For while we live, we are always being given up to death for Jesus' sake, so that the life of Jesus may be made visible in our mortal flesh.... [W]e know that the one who raised the Lord Jesus will raise us also with Jesus, and will bring us with you into his presence.

2 CORINTHIANS 4:8–11, 14

PRAYER

Lord Jesus, it is so hard to make sense of all the suffering in the world. While I realize that suffering is part of the human condition, I do not always understand why it comes into my own life. Sometimes it is too much to handle. Help be to remember that you have taken all of human suffering upon yourself on the cross. I unite my suffering with yours so that I might share in your own redemptive suffering.

LENTEN ACTION

Patiently bear with any suffering you may experience today, offer it to Christ, and view it as a sharing in his redemptive suffering.

DAY 26

Fourth Sunday of Lent

HAPPINESS COMES FROM SAYING "YES" TO GOD

Only Jesus knows what is in your hearts and your deepest desires. Only He, who has loved you to the end (see John 13,1), can fulfill your aspirations. His are words of eternal life, words that give meaning to life. No one apart from Christ can give you true happiness. By following the example of Mary, you should know how to give Him your unconditional "yes." There is no place in your lives for selfishness or laziness. Now more than ever it is crucial that you be "watchers of the dawn," the lookouts who announce the light of dawn and the new springtime of the Gospel of which the buds can already be seen. Humanity is in urgent need of the witness of free and courageous people who dare to go against the tide and proclaim with vigor and enthusiasm their personal faith in God, Lord and Savior.

You are also aware, my dear friends, that this mission is not easy. It becomes absolutely impossible if one counts only on oneself. But "what is impossible with men is possible for God" (Luke 18:27; 1:37).

MESSAGE FOR THE 18TH WORLD YOUTH DAY (APRIL 13, 2003), FROM THE VATICAN, MARCH 8, 2003

MARY'S "YES"

The angel said to her, "Do not be afraid, Mary, for you have found favor with God. And now, you will conceive in your womb and bear a son, and you will name him Jesus.... Mary said to the angel, "How can this be, since I am a virgin?" The angel said to her, "The Holy Spirit will come upon you, and the power of the Most High will overshadow you; therefore the child to be born will be holy; he will be called Son of God. And now, your relative Elizabeth in her old age has also conceived a son; and this is the sixth month for her who was said to be barren. For nothing will be impossible with God." Then Mary said, "Here am I, the servant of the Lord; let it be with me according to your word." Then the angel departed from her.

LUKE 1:30–31, 34–38

PRAYER

Lord, when things are going smoothly in my life, I find it comfortable and easy to follow your will. When things are not going so well, I want to take control and do things my way. Ultimately, however, I know that I will obtain peace in my life only by being unconditionally obedient to you. This Lenten season, help me to grow in my willingness to say "yes" to whatever you ask of me, even when I am afraid.

LENTEN ACTION

Identify an area of your life where you feel that you are resisting God's will. Make an effort to say "yes" in that area.

DAY 27

Monday of the Fourth Week of Lent

FINDING YOURSELF IN CHRIST

The man who wishes to understand himself thoroughly—and not just in accordance with immediate, partial, often superficial, and even illusory standards and measures of his being—he must with his unrest, uncertainty and even his weakness and sinfulness, with his life and death, draw near to Christ. He must, so to speak, enter into him with all his own self, he must "appropriate" and assimilate the whole of the reality of the Incarnation and Redemption in order to find himself. If this profound process takes place within him, he then bears fruit not only of adoration of God, but also of deep wonder at himself. How precious must man be in the eyes of the Creator, if he "gained so great a Redeemer" (*Exsultet* at the Easter Vigil), and if God "gave his only Son" in order that man "should not perish but have eternal life" (sec John 3:16).

REDEMPTOR HOMINIS (THE REDEEMER OF MAN), MARCH 4, 1979

LIVING IN CHRIST

"I am the vine, you are the branches. Those who abide in me and I in them bear much fruit, because apart from me you can do nothing. Whoever does not abide in me is thrown away like a branch and withers; such branches are gathered, thrown into the fire, and burned. If you abide in me, and my words abide in you, ask for whatever you wish, and it will be done for you. My Father is glorified by this, that you bear much fruit and become my disciples."

JOHN 15:5–8

PRAYER

Christ, you are my life. I have meaning only insofar as I unite myself to you. You have shown me the path to life in a world that often seems devoid of meaning. If I want to see the person I am called to become, if I want to become fully human, I only need to look at you. By the outpouring of your self-giving love on the cross, you have shown me the great dignity to which I am called as a child of God. How much you have loved me!

LENTEN ACTION

Take a moment to reflect on how special you must be in God's eyes, given the fact that God sent his only Son to show you the path of life. Do something to make someone else in your life feel special today.

DAY 28

Tuesday of the Fourth Week of Lent

FREED BY THE TRUTH OF CHRIST

*J*esus Christ meets the man of every age, including our own, with the same words: "You will know the truth, and the truth will make you free" (John 8:32). These words contain both a fundamental requirement and a warning: the requirement of an honest relationship with regard to truth as a condition for authentic freedom, and the warning to avoid every kind of illusory freedom, every superficial unilateral freedom, every freedom that fails to enter into the whole truth about man and the world. Today also, even after two thousand years, we see Christ as the one who brings man freedom based on truth, frees man from what curtails, diminishes and as it were breaks off this freedom at its root, in man's soul, his heart and his conscience.

REDEMPTOR HOMINIS (THE REDEEMER OF MAN), MARCH 4, 1979

LISTENING TO THE TRUTH

Pilate asked him, "So you are a king?" Jesus answered, "You say that I am a king. For this I was born, and for this I came into the world, to testify to the truth. Everyone who belongs to the truth listens to my voice."

JOHN 18:37

PRAYER

Jesus, I hear so many conflicting messages in the world. Many different voices tell me that they know the way to true peace, happiness, fulfillment, and freedom. But you have told me that you, the Truth, are the only way to peace and freedom. Lead me in your ways, Lord, so that I might truly be free.

LENTEN ACTION

Make a conscious effort to monitor the messages that you receive from the various forms of media that constantly bombard you with messages (some subtle, some not-so-subtle) about what will make you happy. Reflect on how these messages conflict with what Jesus says about what will bring true happiness and freedom.

DAY 29

Wednesday of the Fourth Week of Lent

FAITHFULNESS

*T*he Passion narrative points out the fidelity of Christ, contrasted with human infidelity. In the hour of his trial, while the disciples and even Peter abandon Jesus (see Matthew 26:56), he remains faithful, willing to pour out his blood to bring to fulfillment the mission the Father has entrusted to him. Beside him is Mary, silent and suffering.

Learn from Jesus and from his—and our—Mother. The real strength of a man lies in the fidelity of his witness to the truth and in his resisting flattery, threats, misunderstandings, blackmail, even harsh and relentless persecution. This is the path on which our Redeemer calls us to follow him.

Only if you are ready to do this, will you become what Jesus expects of you, that is, "the salt of the earth" and "the light of the world" (Matthew 5:13 14).

HOMILY, MARCH 24, 2002 (PALM SUNDAY), 17TH WORLD YOUTH DAY

STAYING WITH JESUS

Then Jesus went with them to a place called Gethsemane; and he said to his disciples, "Sit here while I go over there and pray." He took with him Peter and the two sons of Zebedee, and began to be grieved and agitated. Then he said to them, "I am deeply grieved, even to death; remain here, and stay awake with me." And going a little farther, he threw himself on the ground and prayed, "My Father, if it is possible, let this cup pass from me; yet not what I want but what you want." Then he came to the disciples and found them sleeping; and he said to Peter, "So, could you not stay awake with me one hour? Stay awake and pray that you may not come into the time of trial; the spirit indeed is willing, but the flesh is weak."

MATTHEW 26:36–41

PRAYER

Lord Jesus, you are eternally faithful. I, however, am weak. Would I have stayed awake with you in the Garden on the night before your death, or would I have fallen asleep like your disciples? Would I have followed you to the foot of the cross like your mother Mary, or would I have abandoned you out of fear like your disciples? Lord, there is so much in the world to lure me away from you. I pray for the strength to be faithful to you.

LENTEN ACTION

Practice being faithful. Keep a commitment you have made even when you feel like backing out.

DAY 30

Thursday of the Fourth Week of Lent

TRANSFIGURATION OF THE HEART

This is a great mystery for the life of the Church, since we should not think that the transfiguration will happen only later after death. The saints' lives and the martyrs' witness teach us that if the transfiguration of the body will occur at the end of time with the resurrection of the flesh, that of the heart takes place now on this earth with the help of grace.

We can ask ourselves: What are "transfigured" men and women like? The answer is very beautiful: they are people who follow Christ in living and dying; who are inspired by him and let themselves be imbued with the grace that he gives us; whose food is to do the Father's will; who let themselves be led by the Spirit;... who love others to the point of shedding their blood for them; who are ready to give him their all without expecting anything in return; who—in a word—live loving and die forgiving.

HOMILY, SUNDAY, MARCH 11, 2001

HEARTS OF FLESH

I will give them one heart, and put a new spirit within them;
I will remove the heart of stone from their flesh and give
them a heart of flesh, so that they may follow my statutes
and keep my ordinances and obey them. Then they shall be
my people, and I will be their God.

EZEKIEL 11:19–20

PRAYER

Change my heart, Lord. Make me a new person. Teach me how to live a life that is motivated only by love. Strengthen me so that I may be willing to make sacrifices in order to follow your will. With a transformed heart, I want to be your effective ambassador to the world.

LENTEN ACTION

Spend five minutes taking a look at your heart. What needs transforming? In what areas is there hardness? In what specific, practical way could you become a more loving person? Go out of your way to perform a loving deed as an ambassador of Christ today.

DAY 31

Friday of the Fourth Week of Lent

EMBRACING THE CROSS

*Y*ou do not fear the cross of Christ. Indeed, you love and venerate it because it is the sign of the Redeemer who died and rose again for us. Those who believe in Jesus, crucified and risen, carry the cross in triumph as an indisputable proof that God is love. With the total gift of himself on the cross, our Savior decisively conquered sin and death. Therefore we joyfully proclaim: "Glory and praise to you, O Christ who has redeemed the world with your Cross."

HOMILY, MARCH 24, 2002 (PALM SUNDAY),
17TH WORLD YOUTH DAY

GLORY IN THE POWER OF THE CROSS

For the message about the cross is foolishness to those who are perishing, but to us who are being saved it is the power of God.

1 CORINTHIANS 1:18

May I never boast of anything except the cross of our Lord Jesus Christ, by which the world has been crucified to me, and I to the world.

GALATIANS 6:14

PRAYER

Lord Jesus, your ignominious death on the cross was a great scandal at the time. Yet today we point to your cross as a sign of glory. On the cross you exemplified your ultimate self-giving love by pouring out your life for the redemption of the world. Through the power of the cross, you conquered sin and death for all time. May I always see glory in the cross. Thank you for the gift of your immeasurable sacrifice and love.

LENTEN ACTION

Jesus showed his love for us through the sacrifice of the cross. Show your love for Jesus and someone else in your life by making a sacrifice for that person today.

DAY 32

Saturday of the Fourth Week of Lent

WHAT KIND OF MESSIAH AM I LOOKING FOR?

*F*or this occasion, I invite you to reflect on the conditions that Jesus asked of those who wanted to be his disciples: *"If anyone wishes to come after me,"* he said, *"he must deny himself and take up his cross daily and follow me"* (Luke 9:23). Jesus is not a Messiah of triumph and power. In fact, he did not free Israel from Roman rule and he never assured it of political glory. As a true Servant of the Lord, he carried out his mission in solidarity, in service, and in the humiliation of death. He is the Messiah who did not fit into any mold and who came without fanfare, and who cannot be "understood" with the logic of success and power, the kind of logic often used by the world to verify its projects and actions.

MESSAGE FOR THE 16TH WORLD YOUTH DAY (APRIL 8, 2001),
FROM THE VATICAN, FEBRUARY 14, 2001

THE MESSIAH MUST SUFFER

Now when Jesus came into the district of Caesarea Philippi, he asked his disciples, "Who do people say that the Son of Man is?" …Simon Peter answered, "You are the Messiah, the Son of the living God." And Jesus answered him, "Blessed are you, Simon son of Jonah! For flesh and blood has not revealed this to you, but my Father in heaven.…"

From that time on, Jesus began to show his disciples that he must go to Jerusalem and undergo great suffering at the hands of the elders and chief priests and scribes, and be killed, and on the third day be raised. And Peter took him aside and began to rebuke him, saying, "God forbid it, Lord! This must never happen to you." But he turned and said to Peter, "Get behind me, Satan! You are a stumbling block to me; for you are setting your mind not on divine things but on human things."

MATTHEW 16:13, 16–17, 21–23

PRAYER

Suffering Messiah, I often come to you when I am in need of a quick fix in my life. Help me to remember that the call to follow you is not always without difficulties but often involves suffering. Before the victory of Easter must come the suffering of the cross. You did not avoid the cross. I must follow you to Jerusalem by bearing my own cross. Teach me that true power is found in laying down my life for others.

LENTEN ACTION

Do not avoid something difficult or uncomfortable today. Face the challenge head-on as a sign of your willingness to suffer with Christ. Rather than asking Jesus to remove this burden from you, ask him for the strength to endure it as a sign of your love for him.

DAY 33

Fifth Sunday of Lent

GOD'S LAW LEADS TO FREEDOM, LOVE, AND LIFE

*T*hose who live "by the flesh" experience God's law as a burden, and indeed as a denial or at least a restriction of their own freedom. On the other hand, those who are impelled by love and "walk by the Spirit" (Galatians 5:16), and who desire to serve others, find in God's Law the fundamental and necessary way in which to practice love as something freely chosen and freely lived out. Indeed, they feel an interior urge—a genuine "necessity" and no longer a form of coercion—not to stop at the minimum demands of the Law, but to live them in their "fullness." This is a still uncertain and fragile journey as long as we are on earth, but it is one made possible by grace, which enables us to possess the full freedom of the children of God (see Romans 8:21) and thus to live our moral life in a way worthy of our sublime vocation as "sons in the Son."

VERITATIS SPLENDOR (THE SPLENDOR OF TRUTH), AUGUST 6, 1993

Striving to Follow God's Law

So I find it to be a law that when I want to do what is good, evil lies close at hand. For I delight in the law of God in my inmost self, but I see in my members another law at war with the law of my mind, making me captive to the law of sin that dwells in my members. Wretched man that I am! Who will rescue me from this body of death? Thanks be to God through Jesus Christ our Lord!

ROMANS 7:21–25

Prayer

Lord, contemporary culture says that your moral laws and precepts are limitations of my freedom. I know, however, that you have given me your law in order to direct me to authentic freedom and to the fullness of life. Your law enhances my dignity by helping me to see my great value as a child of God. It leads me in becoming the healthy, happy, fully-human person you want me to be. Help me to see your law not as a limitation, but as a gift.

Lenten Action

Take a look at the Ten Commandments and/or other teachings of the Church. Ask yourself if you see God's law more as a restriction or as a gift. Reflect on how God's law might be seen as leading to greater freedom in your life.

DAY 34

Monday of the Fifth Week of Lent

FALLING IN LOVE WITH GOD THROUGH PRAYER

We have to learn to pray: as it were learning this art ever anew from the lips of the Divine Master himself, like the first disciples: "Lord, teach us to pray!" (Luke 11:1). Prayer develops that conversation with Christ which makes us his intimate friends: "Abide in me and I in you" (John 15:4). This reciprocity is the very substance and soul of the Christian life, and the condition of all true pastoral life....

Yes, dear brothers and sisters, our Christian communities must become genuine "schools" of prayer, where the meeting with Christ is expressed not just in imploring help but also in thanksgiving, praise, adoration, contemplation, listening and ardent devotion, until the heart truly "falls in love."

NOVO MILLENNIO INEUNTE
(AT THE BEGINNING OF THE THIRD MILLENNIUM), JANUARY 6, 2001

PERSISTENCE IN PRAYER

Then Jesus told them a parable about their need to pray always and not to lose heart. He said, "In a certain city there was a judge who neither feared God nor had respect for people. In that city there was a widow who kept coming to him and saying, 'Grant me justice against my opponent.' For a while he refused; but later he said to himself, 'Though I have no fear of God and no respect for anyone, yet because this widow keeps bothering me, I will grant her justice, so that she may not wear me out by continually coming.'" And the Lord said, "Listen to what the unjust judge says. And will not God grant justice to his chosen ones who cry to him day and night? Will he delay long in helping them? I tell you, he will quickly grant justice to them. And yet, when the Son of Man comes, will he find faith on earth?"

LUKE 18:1–8

PRAYER

Lord, teach me how to pray. As with any relationship, ours too requires communication. Remind me that I do not have to do all the talking and that prayer involves putting myself in your presence and listening to you. Make me mindful that in my prayer I need not only ask for my wants and needs, but that I also need to praise you. May the communication of my prayer strengthen our friendship so that I may come to love you more deeply. You have asked me to be persistent in prayer. Inspired by this request, I vow to speak with you more frequently.

LENTEN ACTION

Make an effort to pray at a time you normally would not. Perhaps while showering, cooking, or driving to or from work.

DAY 35

Tuesday of the Fifth Week of Lent

SUSTAINED BY FAITH AND HOPE

Faith helps us to discover the signs of God's loving presence in creation, in people, in the events of history and above all in the work and message of Christ, as he inspires people to look beyond themselves, beyond appearances, towards that transcendence where the mystery of God's love for every creature is revealed. ...Through the virtue of hope, Christians bear witness to the fact that, beyond all evil and beyond every limit, history bears within itself a seed of good which the Lord will cause to germinate in its fullness. They, therefore, look to the new millennium without fear, and face the challenges and expectations of the future in the confident certainty which is born of faith in the Lord's promise.

LENTEN MESSAGE 2000

Man cannot live without hope. Many hopes go down when they crash against the rocks of life. However Christian hope "does not disappoint" because it is based on the solid foundation of faith in the love of God revealed in Christ.

HOMILY AT THE ROMAN PARISH OF ST. GELASIUS, MARCH 3, 2002
(THIRD SUNDAY OF LENT)

PERSEVERING IN FAITH AND HOPE

And you who were once estranged and hostile in mind, doing evil deeds, he has now reconciled in his fleshly body through death, so as to present you holy and blameless and irreproachable before him—provided that you continue securely established and steadfast in the faith, without shifting from the hope promised by the gospel that you heard, which has been proclaimed to every creature under heaven.

COLOSSIANS 1:21–23A

PRAYER

Lord, my Lenten journey can often become discouraging. The troubles of my own life can weigh me down. At times there seems to be so much wrong with the world that I don't really know if good will ever triumph over evil. Strengthen my faith so that I may see your presence in the world rest assured that you are ultimately in control of things. Never let the fire of my hope in you be extinguished, for without it, I could not go on.

LENTEN ACTION

Make a special effort to use the eyes of faith to see the presence of God somewhere in the world where earlier you had not been aware of his presence.

DAY 36

Wednesday of the Fifth Week of Lent

SUFFERING AS OPPORTUNITY FOR GOD TO MANIFEST HIS POWER

Those who share in Christ's sufferings have before their eyes the paschal mystery of the cross and resurrection, in which Christ descends, in a first phase, to the ultimate limits of human weakness and impotence: indeed, he dies nailed to the cross. But if at the same time in this weakness there is accomplished his lifting up, confirmed by the power of the resurrection, then this means that the weaknesses of all human sufferings are capable of being infused with the same power of God manifested in Christ's cross. In such a concept, to suffer means to become particularly susceptible, particularly open to the working of the salvific powers of God, offered to humanity in Christ. In him God has confirmed his desire to act especially through suffering, which is man's weakness and emptying of self, and he wishes to make his power known precisely in this weakness and emptying of self. This also explains the exhortation in the First Letter of Peter: "Yet if one suffers as a Christian, let him not be ashamed, but under that name let him glorify God" (1 Peter 4:16).

SALVIFICI DOLORIS (ON THE CHRISTIAN MEANING OF SUFFERING),
FEBRUARY 11, 1984

CHRIST'S SAVING POWER AMID SUFFERING

Then suddenly a woman who had been suffering from hemorrhages for twelve years came up behind him and touched the fringe of his cloak, for she said to herself, "If I only touch his cloak, I will be made well." Jesus turned, and seeing her he said, "Take heart, daughter; your faith has made you well." And instantly the woman was made well.

MATTHEW 9:20–22

PRAYER

Christ, you demonstrated your power and love by laying down your own life and suffering on the cross. Now, you will to reveal your saving power through my own suffering. Amid my suffering, I have no one to turn to but you. As I turn to you in need, help me to see suffering as an opportunity for you to reveal your strength, mercy, and love.

LENTEN ACTION

Reflect on how God has made known his strength, mercy, and love through your own suffering or that of another.

DAY 37

Thursday of the Fifth Week of Lent

SUFFERING AS AN INVITATION TO REACH OUT TO OTHERS

The parable of the Good Samaritan belongs to the gospel of suffering. For it indicates what the relationship of each of us must be towards our suffering neighbor. We are not allowed to "pass by on the other side" indifferently; we must "stop" beside him. Everyone who stops beside the suffering of another person, whatever form it may take, is a Good Samaritan. This stopping does not mean curiosity but availability. It is like the opening of a certain interior disposition of the heart....

Nevertheless, the Good Samaritan of Christ's parable does not stop at sympathy and compassion alone. They become for him an incentive to actions aimed at bringing help to the injured man. In a word, then, a Good Samaritan is one who brings help in suffering, whatever its nature may be.

SALVIFICI DOLORIS
(ON THE CHRISTIAN MEANING OF SUFFERING), FEBRUARY 11, 1984

THE GOOD SAMARITAN

Jesus replied, "A man was going down from Jerusalem to Jericho, and fell into the hands of robbers, who stripped him, beat him, and went away, leaving him half dead. Now by chance a priest was going down that road; and when he saw him, he passed by on the other side. So likewise a Levite, when he came to the place and saw him, passed by on the other side. But a Samaritan while traveling came near him; and when he saw him, he was moved with pity. He went to him and bandaged his wounds, having poured oil and wine on them. Then he put him on his own animal, brought him to an inn, and took care of him. The next day he took out two denarii, gave them to the innkeeper, and said, 'Take care of him; and when I come back, I will repay you whatever more you spend.' Which of these three, do you think, was a neighbor to the man who fell into the hands of the robbers?" He said, "The one who showed him mercy." Jesus said to him, "Go and do likewise."

LUKE 10:30–37

PRAYER

Lord Jesus, the suffering of others calls me out of my own narcissism to give of myself. Help me to reach out, to be with, and to help others who suffer even if doing so may be inconvenient for me.

LENTEN ACTION

Take time to reach out to someone who is suffering. Share your love by being present to him or her—in person, over the phone, or with a letter. Help to comfort him or her in anyway you can.

DAY 38

Friday of the Fifth Week of Lent

FOLLOWING THE WAY OF CHRIST

If anyone wishes to come after me, let him deny himself and take up his cross daily and follow me (Luke 9:23). These words denote the radicality of a choice that does not allow for hesitation or second thoughts. It is a demanding requirement that unsettled even the disciples and that, throughout the ages, has held back many men and women from following Christ. But precisely this radicality has also produced admirable examples of sanctity and martyrdom that strengthened and confirmed the way of the Church. Even today these words are regarded as a stumbling block and folly (see 1 Corinthians 1:22–25). Yet they must be faced, because the path outlined by God for his Son is the path to be undertaken by the disciple who has decided to follow Jesus. There are not two paths, but only one: the one trodden by the Master.

MESSAGE FOR THE 16TH WORLD YOUTH DAY (APRIL 8, 2001),
FROM THE VATICAN, FEBRUARY 14, 2001

THE ONE WAY

Thomas said to him, "Lord, we do not know where you are going. How can we know the way?" Jesus said to him, "I am the way, and the truth, and the life. No one comes to the Father except through me.

JOHN 14:5–6

PRAYER

Lord, you ask me to follow you wholeheartedly and with complete trust. I know that the path to which you call me is not an easy way. It involves facing hardships head-on and laying down my life for others. Yet I am inspired by the fact that you don't call me to anything that you yourself were not willing to endure. Lead me on the one way—your way—Lord, especially when I am most reluctant to follow you.

LENTEN ACTION

What is the cross that Christ is asking you to carry today? Attempt to embrace it with less reluctance then you may have in the past. Remind yourself that you are following the way of Christ that leads to true life. List five things that stop you from following Christ.

DAY 39

Saturday of the Fifth Week of Lent

AVOIDING IDOLATRY

*B*e worshippers of the only true God, giving him pride of place in your lives! Idolatry is an ever-present temptation. Sadly, there are those who seek the solution to their problems in religious practices that are incompatible with the Christian faith. …[I]t is dangerous to accept the fleeting ideas of the sacred which present God in the form of cosmic energy, or in any other manner that is inconsistent with Catholic teaching.

…[D]o not yield to false illusions and passing fads which so frequently leave behind a tragic spiritual vacuum! Reject the seduction of wealth, consumerism and the subtle violence sometimes used by the mass media. Worshipping the true God is an authentic act of resistance to all forms of idolatry. Worship Christ: he is the Rock on which to build your future.

MESSAGE FOR THE 20TH WORLD YOUTH DAY 2005 (AUGUST 21, 2005), FROM CASTEL GANDOLFO, AUGUST 6, 2004

MAKING OUR OWN GODS

When the people saw that Moses delayed to come down from the mountain, the people gathered around Aaron, and said to him, "Come, make gods for us, who shall go before us; as for this Moses, the man who brought us up out of the land of Egypt, we do not know what has become of him." Aaron said to them, "Take off the gold rings that are on the ears of your wives, your sons, and your daughters, and bring them to me." So all the people took off the gold rings from their ears, and brought them to Aaron. He took the gold from them, formed it in a mold, and cast an image of a calf; and they said, "These are your gods, O Israel, who brought you up out of the land of Egypt!" When Aaron saw this, he built an altar before it; and Aaron made proclamation and said, "Tomorrow shall be a festival to the LORD." They rose early the next day, and offered burnt offerings and brought sacrifices of well-being; and the people sat down to eat and drink, and rose up to revel.

EXODUS 32:1–6

PRAYER

God of all creation, sometimes I turn to things besides you to give me comfort, security, and meaning. In effect, I worship these things and make them my "gods." Help me to acknowledge you as the one and only true God who gives all meaning, purpose, and direction to my life.

LENTEN ACTION

Take one step to demonstrate your commitment to God and your desire to rid your life of false gods. For example, if the possession of material goods has become a god for you, deny yourself the purchase of something you would like to buy and make a contribution to the needy.

DAY 40

Passion Sunday

WHERE DO I STAND?

*H*owever, faith in Christ can never be taken for granted. The reading of his Passion sets us before Christ, living in his Church. The Easter Mystery that we will relive during the days of Holy Week is always present. Today we are contemporaries of the Lord and, like the multitude in Jerusalem, like the disciples and the women, we are called to decide if we are to be with him, or flee, or just be spectators at his death.

Every year in Holy Week the curtain rises once again on the great scene in which the definitive drama is decided, not only for one generation, but for all humanity and for each one.

HOMILY, MARCH 24, 2002 (PALM SUNDAY),
17TH WORLD YOUTH DAY

DENIAL

Now Peter was sitting outside in the courtyard. A servant-girl came to him and said, "You also were with Jesus the Galilean." But he denied it before all of them, saying, "I do not know what you are talking about." When he went out to the porch, another servant-girl saw him, and she said to the bystanders, "This man was with Jesus of Nazareth." Again he denied it with an oath, "I do not know the man." After a little while the bystanders came up and said to Peter, "Certainly you are also one of them, for your accent betrays you." Then he began to curse, and he swore an oath, "I do not know the man!" At that moment the cock crowed. Then Peter remembered what Jesus had said: "Before the cock crows, you will deny me three times." And he went out and wept bitterly.

MATTHEW 26:69–75

STANDING FIRM

Keep alert, stand firm in your faith, be courageous, be strong.

1 CORINTHIANS 16:13

PRAYER

Lord Jesus, each day you ask me to make a choice: Am I with you or not? I am forced to confront my own reluctance and fear. I ask myself: *When you need me to stand by you, do I stand firmly with you in spite of the difficulties and sufferings I know may be involved?* Help me as I strive always to be faithful to you.

LENTEN ACTION

Reflect on the story of the Passion. Place yourself in the story. Be honest with yourself and think about what you would have done as one of Jesus' followers.

DAY 41

Monday of Passion Week

GOD'S LOVE OUTPOURED ON THE CROSS

The cross on Calvary, the cross upon which Christ conducts His final dialogue with the Father, emerges from the very heart of the love that man, created in the image and likeness of God, has been given as a gift, according to God's eternal plan. God, as Christ has revealed Him, does not merely remain closely linked with the world as the Creator and the ultimate source of existence. He is also Father: He is linked to man, whom He called to existence in the visible world, by a bond still more intimate than that of creation. It is love which not only creates the good but also grants participation in the very life of God: Father, Son and Holy Spirit. For he who loves desires to give himself.

DIVES IN MISERICORDIA (RICH IN MERCY),
NOVEMBER 30, 1980

GOD'S ABUNDANT LOVE

God's love was revealed among us in this way: God sent his only Son into the world so that we might live through him. In this is love, not that we loved God but that he loved us and sent his Son to be the atoning sacrifice for our sins. Beloved, since God loved us so much, we also ought to love one another. No one has ever seen God; if we love one another, God lives in us, and his love is perfected in us.

1 JOHN 4:9–12

PRAYER

All-loving Father, you are not distant, but you call me into your very own life. To demonstrate your great love for me, you have sent your Son to bring me into union with you. In the greatest demonstration of love, Jesus was even willing to die on the cross. My mind cannot grasp such an outpouring of love. May the cross always serve as a reminder of your great love for me and your desire to draw me into communion with you.

LENTEN ACTION

Wear a crucifix or carry one in your pocket today as a reminder of God's great love for you as demonstrated through Christ on the cross.

DAY 42

Tuesday of Passion Week

WAY OF CROSS IS WAY OF LIFE

The "way of life" continues and renews the mind of Christ in us and becomes the way of faith and conversion. It is indeed the way of the cross....

There is a widespread culture of the ephemeral that only attaches value to whatever is pleasing or beautiful, and it would like us to believe that it is necessary to remove the cross in order to be happy. The ideal presented is one of instant success, a fast career, sexuality separated from any sense of responsibility, and ultimately, an existence centered on self-affirmation, often bereft of respect for others.

Open your eyes and observe well…: this is not the road that leads to true life, but it is the path that sinks into death. Jesus said: *Whoever wishes to save his life will lose it, but whoever loses his life for my sake will save it.* Jesus leaves us under no illusions: "*What profit is there for one to gain the whole world yet lose or forfeit himself?"* (Luke 9:24–25). With the truth of his words that sound hard but fill the heart with peace, Jesus reveals the secret of how to live a true life.

MESSAGE FOR THE 16TH WORLD YOUTH DAY (APRIL 18, 2001), FROM THE VATICAN, FEBRUARY 14, 2001

LIVING FOR GOD

Do not be deceived; God is not mocked, for you reap whatever you sow. If you sow to your own flesh, you will reap corruption from the flesh; but if you sow to the Spirit, you will reap eternal life from the Spirit. So let us not grow weary in doing what is right, for we will reap at harvest time, if we do not give up. So then, whenever we have an opportunity, let us work for the good of all, and especially for those of the family of faith.

GALATIANS 6:7–10

PRAYER

Lord Jesus, I live in a world that often urges me to avoid discomfort and to seek pleasure at all costs. Yet you have told me that I will only find real meaning in my life by laying down my life in service to others—as you have done. It is in giving of myself and following your way of the cross that I ultimately find myself. Be at my side, Lord, as I face the difficulties of doing what is right, not what is easy.

LENTEN ACTION

Make a sacrifice for someone today. Lay down your own will in order to do God's will in reaching out to someone else. Reflect on whether or not you really show respect for those around you. Today make a special effort to be respectful of those you encounter.

DAY 43

Wednesday of Passion Week

PERSEVERING TO THE END MOTIVATED
BY THE LOVE OF CHRIST

I count everything as loss because of the surpassing worth of knowing Christ Jesus my Lord (Philippians 3: 8). To know Christ! On this last stage of our Lenten journey we are encouraged even more by the liturgy to deepen our knowledge of Jesus, to contemplate his suffering and merciful face, and to prepare ourselves to experience the splendor of his resurrection. We cannot remain on the surface. We must have a deep, personal experience of the richness of Christ's love. Only in this way, as the Apostle says, can we *know him and the power of his resurrection, and may share his sufferings, becoming like him in his death, that if possible [we] may attain the resurrection from the dead* (Philippians 3:10).

HOMILY AT THE ROMAN PARISH OF OUR LADY OF SUFFRAGE
AND ST. AUGUSTINE OF CANTERBURY, APRIL 1, 2001

THE UNCONQUERABLE LOVE OF CHRIST

If God is for us, who is against us? He who did not withhold his own Son, but gave him up for all of us, will he not with him also give us everything else? Who will bring any charge against God's elect? It is God who justifies. Who is to condemn? It is Christ Jesus, who died, yes, who was raised, who is at the right hand of God, who indeed intercedes for us. Who will separate us from the love of Christ? Will hardship, or distress, or persecution, or famine, or nakedness, or peril, or sword?…No, in all these things we are more than conquerors through him who loved us. For I am convinced that neither death, nor life, nor angels, nor rulers, nor things present, nor things to come, nor powers, nor height, nor depth, nor anything else in all creation, will be able to separate us from the love of God in Christ Jesus our Lord.

ROMANS 8:31–39

PRAYER

Lord Jesus, draw near to me and inspire me with your love so that I might persevere to the end of my Lenten journey. I long to enter into a deeper relationship with you, to know you better, to love you more. That is the ultimate goal of this journey. While I dread what is coming as we draw near to Jerusalem and Good Friday, I know that I can face anything when I am united with you and supported by your love. Be with me, Lord, so that I may ultimately share in the joy of your resurrection.

LENTEN ACTION

Christ's love is indomitable. Do you really believe this? What do you fear that might separate you from Christ's love? Take five to ten minutes. Consciously turn that fear over to Jesus. Celebrate Christ's unconquerable love for you by allowing yourself to rest assured in his love. Contemplate how Christ has manifested his love for you.

Also, reflect on what you hoped to achieve and experience this Lenten season. What concrete step can you take today to bring yourself closer to that goal? If there is something you have put off doing to achieve this goal, do it!

DAY 44

Holy Thursday

ENTERING THE UPPER ROOM

On the eve of his passion and death, the Lord Jesus wanted to gather his Apostles around him once again to entrust his last instructions to them and to give them the supreme witness of his love.

Let us also enter the large upper room furnished and ready (Mark 14:15), and dispose ourselves to listen to the most intimate thoughts that he wants to confide to us; in particular, let us be ready to receive the act and the gift that he has prepared in view of this final meeting.

So, while they are eating, Jesus rises from the table and begins to wash the disciples' feet. At first Peter resists, then he understands and accepts. We too are asked to understand: the first thing the disciple must do is to prepare himself to listen to the Lord, opening his heart to accept the initiative of his love. Only then will he be invited, in turn, to do what the Teacher did. He too must be committed to "washing the feet" of his brothers and sisters, expressing in gestures of mutual service that love which is the synthesis of the whole Gospel (see John 13:1–20).

Also during the Supper, knowing that his "hour" had now come, Jesus blesses and breaks the bread, then gives it to the Apostles saying: *This is my body*, he does the same with the cup: *This is my blood.* And he commands them: *Do this in remembrance of me* (1 Corinthians 11:24–25). Truly this is the witness of love taken *to the end* (John 13:1). Jesus gives himself as food to his disciples to become one with them. Once again the "lesson" emerges that we must learn: the first thing to do is to open our hearts to welcoming the love of Christ. It is his initiative: it is his love that enables us, in turn, to love our brethren.

Therefore, the washing of the feet and the sacrament of the Eucharist: two expressions of one and the same mystery of love entrusted to the disciples, so that, Jesus says, *as I have done... so also must you do* (John 13:15).

HOMILY, MASS OF THE LORD'S SUPPER (HOLY THURSDAY),
APRIL 17, 2003

LOVING ONE ANOTHER AS CHRIST HAS LOVED US

I give you a new commandment, that you love one another. Just as I have loved you, you also should love one another. By this everyone will know that you are my disciples, if you have love for one another."

JOHN 13:34–35

PRAYER

Lord Jesus, you have given me the gift of yourself in the Eucharist. Through this outpouring of your love, you also compel me to give the gift of myself to others. Nourished by the Eucharist, may I always find the strength and courage to devote myself for the service of others.

LENTEN ACTION

Tell someone that you love him or her today. In thanksgiving for all that God has given you, perform an act of service. Give up some of your own time and offer to help a friend or family member in whatever way you can. Go a step further and help a stranger by committing even a small amount of time to volunteer at a hospital, hospice, or social service agency. If you have been putting off making such a commitment, do it today.

Good Friday

WHY GOOD FRIDAY IS "GOOD"

*I*n the acute pain of the Suffering Servant we already hear the triumphant cry of the Risen Lord. Christ on the cross is the King of the new people ransomed from the burden of sin and death. However twisted and confused the course of history may appear, we know that, by walking in the footsteps of the Crucified Nazarene, we shall attain the goal. Amid the conflicts of a world often dominated by selfishness and hatred, we, as believers, are called to proclaim the victory of Love. Today, Good Friday, we testify to the victory of Christ Crucified....

Yes, we adore you, Lord, lifted up upon the cross between heaven and earth, the sole Mediator of our salvation. Your cross is the banner of our victory!

WAY OF THE CROSS AT THE COLISEUM, MARCH 29, 2002
(GOOD FRIDAY)

THE VICTORY OVER SIN AND DEATH

When this perishable body puts on imperishability, and this mortal body puts on immortality, then the saying that is written will be fulfilled:
"Death has been swallowed up in victory."
"Where, O death, is your victory?
Where, O death, is your sting?"
The sting of death is sin, and the power of sin is the law. But thanks be to God, who gives us the victory through our Lord Jesus Christ.

1 CORINTHIANS 15:54–57

PRAYER

Lord Jesus, on the surface it is hard to find anything "good" about this day. Yet I know that it was through your suffering and death on the cross that you obtained our salvation and victory over sin and death. Today, we commemorate the victory of your love in a world that is in so much need of it. That certainly is something "good"! Thank you for the gift of your sacrifice—a gift that is beyond all comprehension. I rejoice in your victory!

LENTEN ACTION

When you make the sign of the cross today, in a special way, think of it as a sign of the victory of Christ's love for you.

DAY 46

Holy Saturday

DEATH CONQUERED ONCE AND FOR ALL

On this night death gives way to life for you too, as for all the baptized. Sin is erased and a new life begins. Persevere to the end in fidelity and love. And do not be afraid when difficulties arise, for "Christ being raised from the dead will never die again; death no longer has dominion over him" (Romans 6:9).

EASTER VIGIL HOMILY, APRIL 14, 2001

LIFE WON BY CHRIST

> *If, because of the one man's trespass, death exercised do-minion through that one, much more surely will those who receive the abundance of grace and the free gift of righ-teousness exercise dominion in life through the one man, Jesus Christ.*
>
> *Therefore just as one man's trespass led to condemna-tion for all, so one man's act of righteousness leads to justi-fication and life for all.*

ROMANS 5:17–18

PRAYER

Lord, tonight we celebrate your resurrection by which you made all things new. No longer are we slaves to sin and death. We are alive in the grace of God. Once in darkness, we now see a great light. You have given us new hope. Because of your victory, we need not fear. I forever praise you and thank you for the marvel-ous deeds of this night. Help me to never loose sight of the sig-nificance of your victory.

LENTEN ACTION

Tonight, light a candle as symbol of the victory of Christ's light over the darkness of sin and death. If possible, light this candle during your prayer time throughout the Easter season.

PART II

~~~~~~

READINGS *for* EASTER

DAY 47

Easter Sunday

NEW BEGINNINGS

*O*n this... [day] of Resurrection everything begins anew; creation regains its authentic meaning in the plan of salvation. It is like a new beginning of history and of the cosmos, because Christ is risen, "the first fruits of those who have fallen asleep" (1 Corinthians 15:20). Christ, the "last Adam," has become "a life-giving spirit" (1 Corinthians 15:45).

The same sin of our forefathers is sung in the Easter Proclamation as *felix culpa*, "O happy fault, which gained for us so great a Redeemer!" Where sin abounded, grace now abounds all the more, and "the stone which the builder rejected has become the corner stone..." (Psalm 118:22) of an indestructible spiritual edifice.

On this holy [day]... a new people is born with whom God has sealed an eternal covenant in the blood of the Word made flesh, crucified and risen.

EASTER VIGIL HOMILY, APRIL 19, 2003

NEW CREATION

So if anyone is in Christ, there is a new creation: everything old has passed away; see, everything has become new! All this is from God, who reconciled us to himself through Christ, and has given us the ministry of reconciliation; that is, in Christ God was reconciling the world to himself, not counting their trespasses against them, and entrusting the message of reconciliation to us.

2 CORINTHIANS 5:17–19

PRAYER

Lord, through your resurrection you have made all things new. Sometimes I find myself going in the wrong direction and I need a new start in my own life. Thank you for giving me a second chance. Help me today, Lord, as I commit anew to following you more closely. Renew me, Lord, and make me part of your new creation.

EASTER ACTION

Are you in a rut? Is there a change you have been wanting to make in your life? Turn over a new leaf in your life today. Write a brief note to yourself as a reminder of this day of transformation.

Monday of Easter Week

PEACE OF THE RESURRECTED CHRIST

*T*he risen Jesus encounters the disciples in the Upper Room and offers them the Easter gifts of peace and mercy.... [I]t is well to understand that true peace springs from a heart that is reconciled, and that we who have experienced the joy of forgiveness must therefore be ready to pardon. The Church, also absorbed in prayer today spiritually in the Upper Room, presents to our Lord the joys and the hopes, the sorrows and the anguish of the whole world. And he offers *Divine Mercy* as an effective remedy, asking his ministers to be his generous and faithful instruments.

REGINA CAELI, APRIL 27, 2003 (2ND SUNDAY OF EASTER)

CHRIST'S GIFT OF PEACE

*"I have said these things to you while I am still with you.
But the Advocate, the Holy Spirit, whom the Father will
send in my name, will teach you everything, and remind
you of all that I have said to you. Peace I leave with you; my
peace I give to you. I do not give to you as the world gives.
Do not let your hearts be troubled, and do not let them be
afraid. You heard me say to you, 'I am going away, and I
am coming to you.' If you loved me, you would rejoice that
I am going to the Father, because the Father is greater than
I. And now I have told you this before it occurs, so that when
it does occur, you may believe."*

JOHN 14:25–29

PRAYER

Christ, your death and resurrection demonstrated the great depths
of divine love and mercy. Because of this love and mercy, I need
not worry. I am in your hands, the hands of the Victor over death
and sin. In a world with so many troubles, I can be at peace in
your gentle, loving care. Thank you for this wondrous gift. May
you ever be at my side as I seek to share the gift of your peace
with others.

EASTER ACTION

Christ has shown mercy and love to you. Show the power of the
resurrection over sin and hatred by doing an act of kindness for
someone who has wronged you or someone with whom you
might not ordinarily get along. Pray for that person at least three
times today. Also, take an uninterrupted moment of silence to
relax in Christ's peace.

DAY 49

Tuesday of Easter Week

EUCHARIST: FOOD FOR THE JOURNEY

*T*he Church draws her life from the Eucharist. This truth does not simply express a daily experience of faith, but recapitulates the heart of the mystery of the Church.... [S]he joyfully experiences the constant fulfillment of the promise: "Lo, I am with you always, to the close of the age" (Matthew 28:20), but in the holy Eucharist, through the changing of bread and wine into the body and blood of the Lord, she rejoices in this presence with unique intensity. Ever since Pentecost, when the Church, the People of the New Covenant, began her pilgrim journey towards her heavenly homeland, the Divine Sacrament has continued to mark the passing of her days, filling them with confident hope....

The Eucharist, as Christ's saving presence in the community of the faithful and its spiritual food, is the most precious possession which the Church can have in her journey through history.

ECCLESIA DE EUCHARISTIA, APRIL 17, 2003

THE BREAKING OF THE BREAD

Now on that same day two of them were going to a village called Emmaus, about seven miles from Jerusalem, and talking with each other about all these things that had happened. While they were talking and discussing, Jesus himself came near and went with them, but their eyes were kept from recognizing him.… As they came near the village to which they were going, he walked ahead as if he were going on. But they urged him strongly, saying, "Stay with us, because it is almost evening and the day is now nearly over." So he went in to stay with them. When he was at the table with them, he took bread, blessed and broke it, and gave it to them. Then their eyes were opened, and they recognized him; and he vanished from their sight.… Then they told what had happened on the road, and how he had been made known to them in the breaking of the bread.

LUKE 24:28–32, 35

PRAYER

Lord Jesus, you have promised that you would never leave my side. There are days of my earthly journey during which it is difficult to move forward. You have given me yourself in the Eucharist as strength for my journey. Let me never take this gift for granted but always be aware of your special presence in this sacrament.

EASTER ACTION

Visit a local church and spend time praying before the Blessed Sacrament. Attend a weekday Mass at least once this week. Could this form of spiritual nourishment become a regular part of your spiritual life?

DAY 50

Wednesday of Easter Week

VICTORY OVER SUFFERING

Saint Paul speaks of various sufferings and, in particular, of those in which the first Christians became sharers "for the sake of Christ." These sufferings enable the recipients of that Letter (see 2 Corinthians 4:8–11, 14) to share in the work of the Redemption, accomplished through the suffering and death of the Redeemer. The eloquence of the cross and death is, however, completed by the eloquence of the resurrection. Man finds in the resurrection a completely new light, which helps him to go forward through the thick darkness of humiliations, doubts, hopelessness and persecution. Therefore the Apostle will also write in the Second Letter to the Corinthians: "For as we share abundantly in Christ's sufferings, so through Christ we share abundantly in comfort too" (2 Corinthians 1:5).

SALVIFICI DOLORIS (ON THE CHRISTIAN MEANING OF SUFFERING),
FEBRUARY 11, 1984

SUFFERING TRANSFORMED

Then I saw a new heaven and a new earth; for the first heaven and the first earth had passed away, and the sea was no more. And I saw the holy city, the new Jerusalem, coming down out of heaven from God, prepared as a bride adorned for her husband. And I heard a loud voice from the throne saying,
> *"See, the home of God is among mortals.*
> *He will dwell with them as their God;*
> *they will be his peoples,*
> *and God himself will be with them;*
> *he will wipe every tear from their eyes.*
> *Death will be no more;*
> *mourning and crying and pain will be no more,*
> *for the first things have passed away."*

REVELATION 21:1–4

PRAYER

Lord Jesus, through your resurrection you showed me that my own pain and suffering in this world is not to end with death. Rather, you showed me the glory that awaits me if I but take up my cross and follow you. I know that my suffering is not in vain if I unite it with your own suffering and draw comfort from you. Be by my side as I await the day when you will dry every tear from my eye.

EASTER ACTION

Be an agent of Christ and demonstrate his victory over suffering by comforting someone who is sad or grieving. Visit, write a letter, or call today to express support.

DAY 51

Thursday of Easter Week

THE HOPE OF THE RESURRECTION

*C*hrist is truly risen! Alleluia! Today too the Church continues to make the same joyful proclamation. *Christ is truly risen!* These words are like a cry of joy and an invitation to hope. If Christ is risen, St. Paul notes, our faith is not in vain. If we have died with Christ, we have risen with him: we must now live as risen people....

Everyone needs this saving Word: to everyone the risen Lord brings it personally. Dear parishioners, share this message of hope with those you meet at home, in school, at the office, in the workplace. Reach out especially to those who are alone, who are suffering and in precarious conditions, the sick and the marginalized. To each and every one of them proclaim: Christ is truly risen!

HOMILY AT THE ROMAN PARISH OF ST. STEPHEN PROTOMARTYR,
APRIL 26, 1998

STRENGTHENED BY HOPE

Therefore, since we are justified by faith, we have peace with God through our Lord Jesus Christ, through whom we have obtained access to this grace in which we stand; and we boast in our hope of sharing the glory of God. And not only that, but we also boast in our sufferings, knowing that suffering produces endurance, and endurance produces character, and character produces hope, and hope does not disappoint us, because God's love has been poured into our hearts through the Holy Spirit that has been given to us.

ROMANS 5:1–5

PRAYER

Lord, while I say I believe that you have risen from the dead, I don't always act as someone who believes in your resurrection. Your resurrection has given all people hope in a world that often appears hopeless and filled with darkness. May I always be a beacon of your resurrection to all those who need it.

EASTER ACTION

Be a beacon of hope today. Make an extra effort to greet everyone you encounter—even strangers—with a smile. Offer a word of encouragement to someone who could use it.

Easter Friday

THE GOSPEL OF LIFE

*T*he Gospel of life is for the whole of human society. To be actively pro-life is to contribute to the renewal of society through the promotion of the common good. It is impossible to further the common good without acknowledging and defending the right to life, upon which all the other inalienable rights of individuals are founded and from which they develop. A society lacks solid foundations when, on the one hand, it asserts values such as the dignity of the person, justice and peace, but then, on the other hand, radically acts to the contrary by allowing or tolerating a variety of ways in which human life is devalued and violated, especially where it is weak or marginalized. Only respect for life can be the foundation and guarantee of the most precious and essential goods of society, such as democracy and peace.

There can be no true democracy without a recognition of

every person's dignity and without respect for his or her rights. Nor can there be true peace unless life is defended and promoted.

EVANGELIUM VITAE (THE GOSPEL OF LIFE), MARCH 25, 1995

CHOOSING LIFE

…I have set before you life and death, blessings and curses. Choose life so that you and your descendants may live, loving the LORD your God, obeying him, and holding fast to him; for that means life to you and length of days, so that you may live in the land that the LORD swore to give to your ancestors, to Abraham, to Isaac, and to Jacob.

DEUTERONOMY 30:19–20

PRAYER

God of Life, you created humans in your image and likeness. Yet I live in a world in which the value of human life is often denigrated. Human dignity is under attack on many different fronts. Through the resurrection of Christ, you have shown that life conquers death. May I strive always to promote respect for the value of life from conception to natural death. Instill in all of our hearts greater respect for the dignity of human life, especially in regards to the weakest and most vulnerable among us.

EASTER ACTION

Do you disregard the dignity of human life? Are you in any way indifferent toward the poor and weakest among us? Do you recognize how your decisions impact both those near you and those in different parts of the world? Commit yourself to working for greater social justice, perhaps by joining an organization that promotes the dignity of human life or by volunteering at your church.

DAY 53

Easter Saturday

RESPONSIBILITY TO SPREAD THE GOOD NEWS

*Y*our contemporaries expect you to be witnesses of the One whom you have met and who gives you life. In your daily lives, be intrepid witnesses of a love that is stronger than death. It is up to you to accept this challenge! Put your talents and your youthful enthusiasm at the service of the proclamation of the Good News. Be the enthusiastic friends of Jesus, who present the Lord to all those who wish to see him, especially those who are farthest away from him. Philip and Andrew brought those "Greeks" to Jesus: God uses human friendship to lead hearts to the source of divine charity. Feel responsible for the evangelization of your friends and all your contemporaries.

MESSAGE FOR THE 19TH WORLD YOUTH DAY (APRIL 4, 2004), FROM THE VATICAN, FEBRUARY 24, 2004

To the Ends of the Earth

Now the eleven disciples went to Galilee, to the mountain to which Jesus had directed them. When they saw him, they worshiped him; but some doubted. And Jesus came and said to them, "All authority in heaven and on earth has been given to me. Go therefore and make disciples of all nations, baptizing them in the name of the Father and of the Son and of the Holy Spirit, and teaching them to obey everything that I have commanded you. And remember, I am with you always, to the end of the age."

MATTHEW 28:16–20

Prayer

Risen Lord, you call me to bring your message of hope and salvation to the world. Sometimes I may be called to do this through my actions; other times I may be called to use words. Your Good News is a treasure that I must share with others. You have shown us the meaning of life and the path to eternal happiness with you. The world is starving for this Good News. It would be wrong for me not to share it with others. Strengthen me to be an effective, energetic witness for you. May I never be ashamed to proclaim your love for all people.

Easter Action

Someone once posed the question: "If you were accused of being a Christian, would there be enough evidence to convict you?" What more could you do to be sure that the answer to this question would be "yes"? Share Christ with someone today. Reach out to someone around you in word or deed in order to add to the evidence that could be used to convict you of being a Christian.

DAY 54

Second Sunday of Easter

CALLED TO GREATNESS

The Resurrection of Christ clearly illustrates that only the measure of good introduced by God into history through the mystery of Redemption is sufficient to correspond fully to the truth of the human being. The Paschal Mystery thus becomes the definitive measure of man's existence in the world created by God. In this mystery, not only is eschatological truth revealed to us, that is to say the fullness of the Gospel, or Good News. There also shines forth a light to enlighten the whole of human existence in its temporal dimension and this light is then reflected onto the created world. Christ, through his resurrection, has, so to speak, "justified" the work of creation, and especially the creation of man. He has "justified" it in the sense that he has revealed the "just measure" of good intended by God at the beginning of human history. This measure is not merely what was provided by him in creation and then compromised by man through sin; it is a superabundant measure, in which the original plan finds a higher realization (see Genesis 3:14–15). In Christ, man is called to a new life, as son in the Son, the perfect expression of God's glory. In the words of Saint Irenaeus, *Gloria Die vivens homo*—"the glory of God is man fully alive" (*Adversus haereses*, IV, 20, 7).

MEMORY AND IDENTITY

TO SHINE AS GOD'S CHILDREN

Blessed be the God and Father of our Lord Jesus Christ, who has blessed us in Christ with every spiritual blessing in the heavenly places, just as he chose us in Christ before the foundation of the world to be holy and blameless before him in love. He destined us for adoption as his children through Jesus Christ, according to the good pleasure of his will, to the praise of his glorious grace that he freely bestowed on us in the Beloved. In him we have redemption through his blood, the forgiveness of our trespasses, according to the riches of his grace that he lavished on us.

EPHESIANS 1:3–8

PRAYER

Lord Jesus, your resurrection indicates the greatness to which I am called. You have shown me that by following you in taking up my cross, I too can rise to new life as a child of God. Send me your Spirit, Lord, to strengthen me as I strive to live up to the great dignity to which you have called me. I want to reflect your light to the world.

EASTER ACTION

Find a small symbol of Easter that you can leave displayed somewhere in your home year-round. Let this symbol remind you of the significance of the resurrection and of the great dignity to which you are called.

Sources and Acknowledgments

Quotes of Pope John Paul II, Days 1–2, 4–7, and 9–53, copyright Libreria Editrice Vaticana.

Quotes of Pope John Paul II, Day 3 and Day 54, *Memory and Identity* (New York: Rizzoli, 2005).

Quote of Pope John Paul II, Day 8, *Crossing the Threshold of Hope*, ed. Vittorio Messori, trans. Jenny McPhee and Martha McPhee (New York: Alfred A. Knopf, 1994).